MUSCLE CARS

THE LEGEND LIVES ON

igloo

Contents

Introduction

It's the sheer simplicty of the Muscle Car that makes it so universally appealing. The recipe is just so straightforward. Take a compact automobile and install an incredibly-powerful engine (preferably a V8) to deliver a tire-frying performance. No auto enthusiast can argue with that one. It's a formula for success that has been tried and tested for 50 years and has created some of the most exciting cars in history. Just mentioning the names Mustang, Charger, GTO, Corvette or Viper sends a shiver down the spine.

The Muscle Car story began in America's post-war boom of the 1950s as inter-brand rivalry in Detroit saw horsepower figures steadily rising through the decade. But these big engines were being fitted to big cars and they didn't have mass-market appeal.

That would all change in 1964 when Pontiac installed a full-size engine into a mid-size car and created the awesome GTO, the first true Muscle Car. And the rest of Detroit followed. Fast. The Ford Mustang, Plymouth Road Runner, Dodge Charger, Plymouth Barracuda and Chevrolet Camaro all appeared before the eager public could pause for breath. Horsepower went through the roof as the cars competed on the streets and on the track. Ford managed to wring 675bhp out of its Cammer V8, the highest power of any Detroit engine ever. Hertz bought up a whole series of Shelby GT350 Mustangs to rent out to weekend racers and Plymouth's Road Runner Superbird and its Dodge Daytona rival brought NASCAR to the streets. It was Muscle Car mania.

But dark clouds were looming. Tough emissions rules and the oil crisis forced automobile manufacturers to rethink. Power outputs fell through the floor during the 1970s and there were plenty of casualties. The Dodge Charger and Challenger, Plymouth Road Runner and Pontiac GTO all fell victim to the

legislation and it looked like the Muscle Car was dead.

Only Pontiac's Firebird Trans Am, Chevrolet's Camaro and Corvette and Ford's Mustang kept the spirit alive. But the truth was that for many years these cars were anything but muscular, offering a lot more show than go.

It was only towards the very end of the 1980s that things were looking up. The survivors were beginning to pack more punch and at least one company was reminiscing about the good old days.

That company was Chrysler. In a bid to re-establish its Dodge and Plymouth brands the designers and engineers had been studying their history. In 1989 the Detroit Auto Show ground to a halt as the wraps came off the Dodge Viper concept car. With its epic V10 engine and muscular lines it was the machine that Muscle Car fans had been dreaming of for two decades.

Dodge put the Viper into production and it was a phenomenal hit. Come 1997 the company was ready to do it again, this time with the Plymouth Prowler – a hot rod for the 21st Century. Performance and style were hot again.

Today Muscle Cars are back with a vengeance and legendary names are reappearing in dealerships, drag strips and ovals. The 2005 C6 Corvette is the most powerful ever, packing 500bhp in S06 trim. Chrysler has brought back the 300 and the Dodge Charger. Ford has revived the Mustang Shelby GT500. It's like the glory days of the 1960s all over again.

The Muscle Cars of the new millennium are faster than ever before and not just able to rip up the quarter-mile, but relish twisty roads too with advanced suspension and the latest electronic driver aids. If that sounds too complicated for die hard Muscle Car fans don't worry, because none of the newcomers has forgotten that basic principle. Horsepower is still the number one priority as the Muscle Car legend lives on.

AMC AMX

AMC's cut-down Javelin was an oddball, but it was the company's best player in the muscle car era

The AMC AMX of 1968 was the only two-seater American sportscar of the time.

Essentially a cut-down version of AMC's Javelin the AMX (American Motors eXperimental), was a foot shorter than its sibling. With rather odd proportions, the AMX was significantly lighter than the Javelin.

With the top-flight 315bhp 390 cubic inch V8 installed, the AMX was a lively performer. Zero to sixty came in just 6.9 seconds and the quarter-mile in

15 seconds. There was a four-speed manual tranny, toughened suspension and bucket seats for two occupants. A 290 and 343 V8 were lesser options.

Land speed racing legend Craig Breedlove set no less than 106 speed records with an AMX in February 1968. In celebration, a special run of 50 Craig Breedlove editions were built. Finished in patriotic red, white and blue, few of these survive today.

A few minor cosmetic changes were made for 1969

but the year is best remembered for the Big Bad AMX, available in bold orange, green and blue color schemes with bumpers that matched.

It also had a Go pack which included power disc brakes, uprated suspension for improved handling and redline tires.

A very limited run of SS cars designed for the drag strip were also produced. Modifications to the 390 cubic inch V8 engine resulted in a claimed power output of 340bhp, but as was often the case in the muscle car

MODEL HISTORY

1968	1969	1970	1971	1974
AMX launched, based on shortened Javelin	*Limited-run SS is the most powerful and most expensive AMX*	*The last two-seater AMX is built*	*AMX is now the top model in the Javelin range*	*AMX production run ends*

era, this was a very conservative estimate. The SS package almost doubled the AMX's sticker price, and only around 50 were sold in the end.

In 1971, the AMC AMX was the name for the top model Javelin. It had a curiously bulbous hood and a choice of two 360 cubic inch V8s with 245 or 290bhp. More power came with the Go package which used a 401 330bhp V8 under the hood and

upgraded the wheels, tires and brakes as part of the deal. 1972 was the last year for the AMX as a muscle car. The entry-level engine had been reduced to a 304 cubic inch unit with a paltry 150bhp.

The AMX continued to be sold until 1974, but its days as a muscle car were long finished.

Specification

Years built	1966-1974
Most powerful model	1969 SS
Engine type	V8
Displacement	401 cid
Transmission	four-speed manual
Power	340bhp
Top speed	120mph

Buick
Gran Sport

Buick's entry to the muscle car fray may have been late but it was a worthy contender

Many see the GTO as the first true muscle car, setting the formula for others to follow: drop a big-block V8 into an intermediate-sized car and sell it at a budget price.

So Buick shoehorned its 401 cubic inch 'nailhead' V8 into its existing Skylark model, bestowing it with 325bhp, to cash in on this new trend. Despite arriving later in the day, the Gran Sport was a strong seller in its first year and Buick was encouraged to hone the car further.

For 1966, the Gran Sport was given a new, hotter 340bhp version of the 401 engine, dropping its quarter mile time by a second to 15.4secs. Buying into the Buick brand wasn't cheap and Gran Sport sales were a lot slower than in its introductory year.

The name was abbreviated in 1967, when the GS 400 arrived with a new, higher-revving 400 cid engine also giving 340bhp. A new three-speed auto transmission and the 260bhp 'junior' GS 340 also saw the light of day and its cut price helped sales.

Then came the Stage One Special Package with a unique 400 cid motor. Although officially rated at 345bhp (just 5bhp more than the regular

MODEL HISTORY

1965
Buick fits 401 cid 'nailhead' engine into Skylark, producing the Gran Sport

1967
New 400 cid V8 introduced, along with the smaller-engined GS 340

1969
Previously fake hood scoopsbecame a functional part of the induction system

1970
The GS 455 is born. In Stage 1 tune with the GSX style pack, it is the ultimate Buick muscle car

1972
Last true Buick GS produced. After this the name became a pale shadow of its former glory

400), the reality was more like 390bhp.

In 1970, the GS 455 had a brand new 455 cubic inch engine to give plenty of go, while the GSX appearance package provided all the show: spoilers, classic body stripes and supersize tires.

The combination made for the ultimate Buick muscle car of all time, when the Stage 1 performance package was specified, giving a hotter

Specification

Years built	1965 to 1975
Most powerful model	1970 GS 455
Engine type	V8
Displacement	455 cu in
Transmission	three-speed automatic
Power	360bhp
Top speed	130mph

cam, bigger valves and a revised carburetor. The company under-rated it at 360bhp, as road testers of the time claimed it was nearer 400bhp!

1971 signalled the beginning of the end for the GS and post-1972, the GS name was shunted. The glory of the muscle car years were long gone.

Buick *Wildcat*

Buick's first attempt at high-performance never shrugged off its luxury image

Buick was not known for its high performance machinery, but this started to change in 1962 when the Wildcat hit the scene.

Part of the Invicta line, the Wildcat Sport Coupe (as it was officially called) benefited from a beefed-up chassis and suspension, and more dragstrip-oriented transmission ratios to make the most of the 401 cid V8 engine's 325bhp. Loaded with luxury, its weight was pumped up to a hefty 4,150 pounds.

During its eight-year lifespan, the Wildcat was given more and more power. The original two-door hardtop body style was also bolstered by a four-door hardtop, a two-door convertible and finally a conventional four-door sedan.

Despite Buick's view of the Wildcat as a sports car, the public thought different; it was the staid-looking sedan that saw the greatest sales success.

In '64, two new optional 425 cid V8s were made available, with 340 and 360bhp, which helped to offset the increased 4,500-pound curb weight.

In 1965 the style changed. The Wildcat shared its sheet metal with its Buick stablemate, the Le Sabre, and lost some of its individuality in the process.

The introduction of the Wildcat Custom, with more luxurious interior trimming, arrived in 1966 along with an optional high performance package. Only 21 owners took up this high-performance 425 cid V8, which was good for 380bhp and 465 lbft of torque with its pair of four-barrel carbs and a dual exhaust to make the gas flow freely.

A more efficient domed combustion chamber in the all-

MODEL HISTORY

1962
First Wildcat introduced as part of Buick's Invicta model line-up, powered by 325bhp 401 cid V8

1963
Sports coupe body style is augmented by a four-door hardtop and two-door convertible

1964
Optional 340 and 360bhp 425 cid V8s introduced along with new four-door sedan

1965
All-new styling sees Wildcat sharing bodyshell with Buick Le Sabre

1970
Final model has most powerful standard engine at 370bhp

new standard 430 cid engine of 1967 raised power to 360bhp, but by '69 the styling was so similar to the Le Sabre that the two were virtually identical. Only the grille, a few body moldings and the steering wheel differed. The Wildcat's lack of identity led to a drop in sales.

Finally, in 1970, the Wilcat went out with a howl, not a whimper. The run-out model featured Buick's all-new 455 cid V8,

producing 370bhp and 510 lbft of torque.

So what was arguably Buick's first performance car ended its days with the most powerful standard engine it ever had.

The flirtation with muscle cars was a short one and Buick reverted to what its buyers loved best; luxury.

Specification

Years built	1962 to 1970
Most powerful model	1970 455
Engine type	V8
Displacement	455 cu in
Transmission	three-speed automatic
Power	370bhp
Top speed	130mph

Chevrolet Camaro

Chevrolet's answer to the Ford Mustang was late, but worth the wait

The Camaro was General Motors' belated response to the Mustang. Two years after Ford's pony car appeared GM released the Camaro. The 1967 Camaro was an instant success.

It came as a hardtop coupe and convertible and could be tailored to each individual customer's requirements. There were four engines, a choice of three basic trim packages and no less than 80 factory options and a further 40 dealer options.

As standard the Camaro came with a 230 cubic inch straight six with 140bhp or a 250 with 155bhp, but of far more interest were the V8s. A 327 came with 295bhp or 275bhp and there was a 350 offered as part of the SS package with 325bhp and then a 396 with 375bhp. The SS also offered unique bumble bee stripes, air intakes on the hood and a blacked out grille. Customers could choose the RS pack which included hidden headlights, revised tail lamps

Mated to a four-speed manual Muncie transmission and with power disc front brakes and competition suspension there was no mistaking this car's breeding. To emphasise this you could add a set of racing stripes.

With a top speed of 140mph the Z-28 was a spectacular way to celebrate the end of 1967. But 1969 would be a big year for the Camaro.

The biggest changes were under the hood. SS customers could opt for one of two ram air systems – one was an aggressive new hood, with a rear-facing

1967 SS pace car (opposite), '79 cars (above) and '69 on the beach (below)

and a higher level of interior trim - or even combine the two packages to get performance with style with an RS/SS. Adding further credibility was the Camaro's role as pace car for the 1967 Indy 500.

By the end of the year there was another option: the Z-28. The Z-28 was a homologation special, built so that the Camaro could go racing in the Trans Am Series, and although its 302 cubic inch motor was officially rated at just 290bhp, this engine threw out closer to 400bhp.

MUSCLE CARS

MODEL HISTORY

1967
Chevrolet launches the Camaro – two years after the Ford Mustang

1969
The most powerful Camaros appear. First the COPO 427 with 450bhp and then the ZL1 with 500bhp

1970
The second generation arrives with European-influenced styling

1971
GM's new regulations strangle power outputs

1980
Power outputs drop throughout the decade, leaving a Z-28 with just 165bhp

air inlet and the other, if you didn't want that power bulge on the bonnet, was a dealer-fit plenum kit.

A new 307 V8 was offered with a modest 200bhp but for extreme performance Chevrolet offered a mighty 427 cub inch unit.

There was a dealer-fit engine that offered up to 450bhp. Ordered through Chevrolet's Central Office Production Order System these COPO were installed by well-known dealers including Yenko Sports Cars of Pennsylvania. Yenko also added rallye wheels and upgraded suspension to create their ultimate Camaro.

But even these COPO cars were put in the shade by Chevrolet's ZL1. This aluminium block engine was rated at 430bhp but was really closer to 500bhp. Designed to compete in NHRA Super Stock drag racing, only a handful were sold as the cost of the engine alone nearly doubled the price of the car.

1971 saw the Camaro's horsepower slashed thanks to emissions regulations. Even the Z-28 was down to 330bhp.

Throughout the 1970s the Camaro's styling was revised to incorporate new Federal bumpers and power steadily declined.

In 1982 the third incarnation

1982
The third incarnation is launched with an embarrassing 90bhp engine as standard

1985
IROC-Z is unveiled and boosts power to 215bhp

1993
The final generation appears. Z28 offers 275bhp

1997
30th anniversary celebrated with a 330bhp SS LT1

2003
Camaro production ends

appeared. More angular styling and an all-new chassis with new suspension were the highlights.

Under the bonnet it was a bit of a disappointment. The entry-level engine was a 2.5-liter (153 cubic inch) four-cylinder unit with a pathetic 90bhp, then there was a 2.8-liter (171 cid) V6 with 112bhp.

Over its ten-year life power did gradually pick up, though. In '85 came the IROC-Z with a more respectable 215bhp. And by 1992 this was boosted to 245bhp bringing some credibility back to the Camaro brand.

For its final generation the 1993 Camaro reclaimed even more street cred. With its aerodynamic new design, revised suspension for improved handling and power levels that once again approached

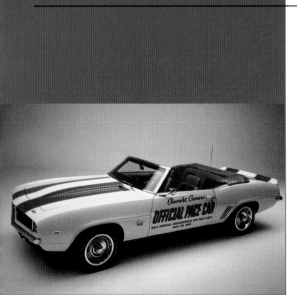

1996 coupe (below) and 35th anniversary specials from 1992 (opposite)

THE ULTIMATE
CAMARO

1969 was undoubtedly the best year to buy a Camaro if you really felt the need for speed. COPO cars modified at big Chevy dealers such as Yenko in Pennsylvania, Nickey in Chicago, Dana in California and Baldwin-Motion in New York produced up to 450bhp. But the factory went further. To compete in the NHRA Super Stock drag class they needed to produce 50 road cars. Fitted with an aluminium block ZL1 engine officially rated at 430bhp, the truth was that this car had more like 500bhp. Even on street tyres and a standard exhaust it could run the standard quarter-mile in 13 seconds. In full race trim it was two seconds faster. But it was expensive. At $4,160 just the engine cost more than a standard SS model and only 69 were made.

those of the 1970s it was the most accomplished Camaro ever. Engines were a 3.4-liter (207 cid) 160bhp V6 or a 5.7-liter (348 cid) 275bhp V8 in the Z-28.

A convertible joined the coupe a year later and in 1996 the SS model returned with a bang, offering 305bhp. Then to celebrate the Camaro's 30th anniversary in 1997 it received the superb LS1 engine from the Corvette offering 330bhp and making it the most powerful model in over 20 years.

The Camaro carried on long enough to celebrate its 35th anniversary with another special edition, but 2002 would mark the end for this once great muscle car.

Specification

Years built	1967 to 2002
Most powerful model	1967 COPO ZL1
Engine type	V8
Displacement	427 cu in
Transmission	four-speed manual, rear-wheel drive
Power	500bhp
Top speed	150mph

1969 coupe (above) and 1977 Z28 (right)

1988 T-Top (above) and 1981 Z28 (left)

2001 convertible (above) and 1993 T-Top (right),

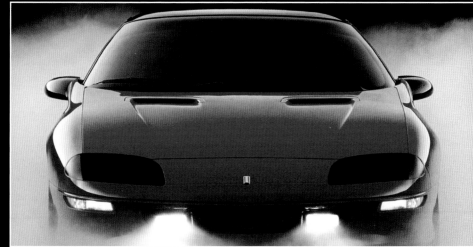

1994 Z28
(above) and
the 1987
collection (left)

Chevrolet
Chevelle SS

Chevy's response to the Pontiac GTO soon overshadowed its rival

Launched in 1964, the Chevelle SS was a fairly plain-looking sedan and , although a 283 cubic inch and 327 V8 were both offered and the maximum output was a sizeable 300bhp, it still fell a long way short of Pontiac's GTO.

Chevrolet reacted quickly. By 1965 the Z-16 Chevelle SS packed 375bhp from its 396 cubic inch V8. Fiercely fast, it could accelerate from

0-60mph in six seconds flat and do the standing quarter mile in less than 15 seconds.

Chevelle was redesigned a year later with a more rounded look and two bonnet scoops that would be a hallmark of the SS.

By 1968 the Chevelle had been redrawn again, with a more aggressive fastback body, although power remained at 375bhp from the highest-rated L78 V8.

MODEL HISTORY

1964	1965	1968	1970	1973
Chevelle SS launched, but lacks punch	*Problem solved thanks to the 375bhp Z-16*	*Major restyle brings a fastback body*	*Chevelle becomes the most powerful muscle car ever*	*Chevelle production run ends*

Even that wasn't enough in the Muscle Car Wars. In '69 Chevrolet released a limited number of very special Chevelles. Known as the COPO (Central Office Production Order), they packed even more punch from a special order engine that was catalogued as L72.

1970 was the Chevelle's finest hour. In went a 402 or 454 cubic inch motor, with the LS6 454 unit producing an epic 450bhp. It was the fastest SS ever and could do the standing quarter-mile in less than 14 seconds.

Having to run on unleaded fuel and meet tough new emissions standards set by GM management meant that the great V8s were strangled and even the highest output engine was down almost 100bhp on the previous year.

It was a big come down for a once great car and sales dropped. By 1973 the Chevelle SS was gone.

Specification

Years built	1964 to 1973
Most powerful model	1970 SS
Engine type	V8
Displacement	454 cu in
Transmission	four-speed manual
Power	450bhp
Top speed	130mph

Chevrolet *Corvette*

The Corvette has been America's Sports Car for more than 50 years

Now in its sixth generation the Chevrolet Corvette has been America's Sports Car for more than 50 years.

Originally shown as a concept car at the General Motors Motorama at New York's Waldorf Astoria hotel in January of 1953, it was launched to the public barely six months later. Penned by legendary GM stylist Harley Earl, the Corvette was a thing of beauty. It was compact and cute, featuring some of Earl's best known party pieces including 'twin pod' rear fenders and 'rocket ship' tail lights plus a snarling toothy grille. Initially only available in Polo White with a red interior, the Corvette was drop dead georgeous.

It also marked a radical departure in production methods. All Corvettes were hand built, based on a shortened Chevrolet passenger car chassis of 102 inches and with those curves created not

and also offered a beige interior option, but mechanically and visually the Corvette was unchanged. Sales picked up to more than 3,000.

But 1955 nearly saw the death of the Corvette. Sales plummeted to just 700 and the money men within GM wanted to axe the car. Then along came racing driver Zora Arkus-Duntov. He believed what the car really needed was more power and better handling. So in went a 265 cubic inch V8 with 195bhp and an optional three-speed manual transmission. At Daytona

1972 Stingray (opposite) 1953 original (top) and 1960 convertible (below)

from beaten metal, but moulded fiberglass. The 'Vette boasted coil sprung wishbone suspension at the front and four-leaf semi-elliptical springs at the rear.

Under the hood was an off-the-shelf 235 cubic inch straight six engine, tricked up with a higher lift cam to produce 150bhp. Chevy's Powerglide two-speed auto transmission was fitted as standard.

The hand-built Corvette cost more than a Cadillac or even an imported Jaguar.

For '54 Chevrolet offered black, blue and red colors

MUSCLE CARS

MODEL HISTORY

1953
Corvette launched.
Highlights include
Harley Earl-
designed fibreglass
body, but a very
high sticker price

1958
Production almost
cancelled.Corvette
saved by Zora
Arkus-Duntov who
fits the first V8

1963
C2 Sting Ray
launched – for
many the most
beautiful
Corvette ever

1968
C3 launched, based
on Mako Shark II
concept car. T-top
introduced

1984
C4 goes on sale.
The hardest
working Corvette
lasts 12 years

Duntov ran the measured mile at 150mph and a legend was born.

Over the next two years the 'Vette really came into its own. A '56 restyle gave birth to the famous scalloped sides. In 1957 came a 283 cubic inch V8 offering 220bhp as standard, but with the 'Fuelie' motor a hefty 283bhp. Enough for the Corvette to crack the quarter mile in 14 seconds.

Between '58 and '62 the styling and speed evolved gradually. By the time the end of the line came for the mark one 'Vette a 327 cubic inch V8 was now standard and horsepower had shot up to 360bhp with the 'Fuelie' motor.

1963 brought the Sting Ray body in convertible or split window coupe styles. For many people this is the ultimate Corvette, and in Z06 race tri it was a major player. Over the four years of the second generation Corvette, handling was uprated, brakes became all-wheel discs and the engine choice was widened to include a number of 327 V8s and a mighty 427. Officially rated at 430bhp, true figures of up to 600bhp were widely talked about.

Based closely on GM's Mako Shark II concept the C3 'Vette made its debut in 1968. New features included a removable

1990

The ZR-1 is unveiled with 375bp – the most powerful Corvette since the 1970s

1996

C5 hits the road and the T-top returns

2001

Zo6 offers 385bhp

2004

C6 arrives with 400bhp as standard

2005

Zo6 is the fastest, most powerful Corvette ever, with 500bhp

T-top for the Stingray coupe and a three-speed automatic gearbox to replace the old two-speed unit.

By 1970 the engine choice was a 350 V8 or a 450 although with 'only' 390bhp offered on the top flight LS5. A year later came the LS6 and power was back up to 430bhp again.

Throughout the Seventies the Corvette was progressively modernised, most notably with the introduction of Federal bumpers in 1974. And in a nod to the oil crisis, the big block V8 disappeared, with only the 350 remaining for the rest of this model's life. The Stingray name also went.

The fourth generation 'Vette had the longest lifespan. The styling was all-new and, although a significant change from the

The C4 (below) was the longest-lived 'Vette. The 2003 C5 celebrated 50 glorious years

THE ULTIMATE
CORVETTE

Born out of tremendous success in the American Le Mans race series the 2006 Z06 is the ultimate Corvette. Its 427 cubic inch V8 packs 500bhp, which means this amazing car can hit zero to sixty in four seconds, hack the quarter mile in less than 12 seconds and top out at more than 190mph.

But there's more to it than just horsepower. The hardtop body is super rigid, the brakes feature 14-inch, cross-drilled discs and there are 18-inch front and 19-inch wheels. The suspension is stiffer and lower than standard and the whole car is wider than a normal C6.

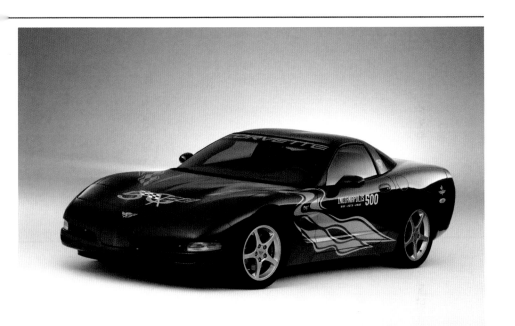

C3, it was the least visually exciting model. A significant moment in the C4's life came in 1990 when a six-speed manual gearbox was introduced and the ZR-1 was launched with its mighty 375bhp. Three years later the ZR-1 was packing 405bhp, although it was only on sale for three years.

In 2004 the sixth generation Corvette hit the streets. Widely regarded as the most sophisticated and best-driving of the bunch, it comes with a six-liter (366 cubic inch) V8 offering 400bhp. Included were such high tech offerings as a Head Up Display, ABS brakes and Active Handling. America's Sports Car is now able to rival the best of European exotica.

Specification

Years built	1953 to date
Most powerful model	2005 Z06
Engine type	V8
Displacement	427 cu in
Transmission	six-speed manual, rear-wheel drive
Power	500bhp
Top speed	190mph+

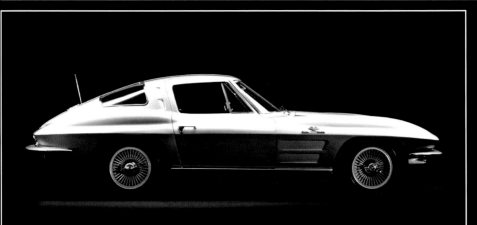

Sting Rays from 1963 (above) and 1965 (right)

1984 C4 *(above) and* 1968 T-top *Stingray (left)*

1996 C4
convertible
(above) and 1973
Stingray hardtop,

2002 C5 (above)
and 2005 C6
(left)

Chevrolet
El Camino

The crazy El Camino brought muscle car madness to the pickup market

Chevrolet first introduced its unique oddball car/truck hybrid in 1959. Based on the Impala, it hardly set any sales records and only lasted two years.

But in 1964 the El Camino was back. Now based on the Chevrolet Chevelle, the El Camino meant business. There was a choice of 283 or 327 cubic inch V8s. Power outputs were respectable, if not awe-inspiring, with the base car offering 195bhp and the top of the line packing 250bhp.

For real muscle El Camino fans would have to wait until 1968 for the arrival of the SS. By now the El Camino looked less truck-like than ever. It was long, low and lean, with its bonnet scoops emphasizing its performance potential.

Like its sister car the Chevelle SS this was a seriously powerful machine, driven by a 396 cubic inch V8 and available in three states of tune. There was 325bhp from the standard SS396, 350bhp from the L34

version and a heavyweight 375bhp from the L78.

1970 saw the El Camino receive the same facelift as the Chevelle, and that brought even more power. The 396 engine was replaced by a 300bhp 350 for the standard unit with a new 402 offering 350 or 375bhp. Not bad. Until you consider the 454 LS6 option that took the El Camino up to an astonishing 450bhp.

This pickup could now run the quarter mile in less than 14

MODEL HISTORY

1959
El Camino first appears, based on the Impala

1964
After a short break it's back and now based on the Chevelle

1968
El Camino SS unveiled with 396 power

1970
The Ultimate El Camino arrives with an astonishing 450bhp.

1983
The final El Camino is built

seconds. Muscle car madness was at its height. The El Camino is probably the most bizarre example of the extreme lengths that car makers went to.

But just as the impending oil crisis and strict new emission rules hit the Chevelle SS, so they hit the El Camino and in 1971 it was massively detuned. Even the LS6 was down to

just 365bhp; less than the L78 of 1969. It marked the beginning of the end.

A year later and the most

Specification

Years built	1959 to 1973
Most powerful model	1970 SS
Engine type	V8
Displacement	454 cu in
Transmission	Turbo-Hydramatic
Power	450bhp
Top speed	130mph

powerful El Camino produced just 270bhp and by the time the final incarnation came along – based now on the Chevy Malibu – there was a maximum of just 245bhp on offer.

The El Camino continued in production until 1983, but never again reached the great heights of 1970.

Chevrolet
Impala SS

The Impala could just be the car that started muscle car mania

Born in 1958 as the highest specification Bel Air, the Impala was Chevrolet's most expensive model. It came as a hardtop or convertible with no less than seven engine options varying from just 145bhp to 315bhp.

A year later the Impala was longer, wider and only a Cadillac offered more outrageous Batmobile styling. 1961 would be a

memorable year thanks to the introduction of the Impala Super Sport or SS. By now the Impala was available with a choice of three 348 cid V8s with 305, 340 or 350bhp plus a mighty 409 offering 360bhp.

In 1962 a pair of four-barrel carbs was added to the huge 409 engine, giving the Impala one horsepower for every cubic inch. By 1963 the Impala packed

MODEL HISTORY

1958
Impala introduced as top of the line Bel Air

1961
Super Sport option goes on sale. Epic 409 engine is most powerful

1969
Impala reaches the end of the road

1994
Impala returns for two years as a rebadged Chevy Caprice

2004
Impala returns again – with front wheel drive!

430bhp with a special Z-11 427 cubic inch lump.

1965 saw a more streamlined look. The 409 engine was swapped for a new 396. A year later the Impala was no longer King of the Hill at Chevrolet due to the arrival of the Caprice and both sales and the car's prestige gradually went into to decline. The last Impala of this generation rolled off the production line in 1969. Chevrolet briefly revived the Impala SS name from 1994 to 1996. A 350 V8 offered 260bhp, but it was a large and staid-looking machine.

The Impala reappeared once more in 2000 with front-wheel drive and even the latest 2005 SS with its 240bhp supercharged V6 engine can hardly be mentioned in the same breath as the original. The Impala's muscle car days are long gone.

Specification

Years built	1958 to date
Most powerful model	1963 SS
Engine type	V8
Displacement	409 cu in
Transmission	four-speed manual
Power	430bhp
Top speed	130mph

Chrysler *300*

Chrysler's luxury 300 started Detroit's horsepower race in 1955 and launched the epic Hemi engine

The Chrysler 300 was responsible for the start of Detroit's horsepower race. This coupe, launched in 1955, came with a 331 cubic inch V8 engine as standard. And as no ordinary V8; it was the first Hemi.

Named after the hemispherical shape of the combustion chambers, it produced 300bhp. Mated to a PowerFlite transmission, the C-300 burnt its special Blue Streak racing tyres when it ran the

flying mile at 127.58mph. This first Chrysler 'letter car' was not cheap. Only 1,725 were built.

A year later the 300B was released. Power now came from a 354 cid Hemi with 340bhp as standard or 355bhp in high

establishing a reputation as a real high performance machine.

For '58 the car was renamed 300D and once more Hemi power was raised. 380bhp was standard and 390bhp came with the optional addition of electronic fuel injection. The innovative system wasn't very reliable and few buyers opted for it. At Bonneville Salt Flats a 300D set a new speed record of 156.387mph.

In '59 the Hemi was replaced by a new Golden Lion 413 cid V8 with 380bhp and a year later a 400bhbp

1955 original (opposite page), 1958 (above) and 2005 (below)

output form. The 300 even achieved close to 140mph in the flying mile.

In 1957, the Hemi packed even more power. With a 392 cid capacity it had 375bhp as standard. A high output version came with 390bhp thanks to a more extreme cam and bigger exhausts. Mated to a four-speed manual transmission the 300B could run the quarter-mile in 17 seconds and crack zero to sixty in just 7.7 seconds. Available as a two-door hardtop or convertible the 300 was

version of the same engine was offered. 1961's 300G was completely restyled. Luxury options and gadgets included a six-way power seat and power door locks.

By the close of 1963 the Chrysler 300 was no more, but the final incarnation, the 300J was the fastest of them all (in standard production form). A new, more aerodynamic body helped it to 142mph.

And that was it for 40 years. But in 2004 Chrysler unveiled a new 300. Just like the original, it packs Hemi power. Voted 2005 Car of the Year by Motor Trend, the latest 300 comes only as a four-door. But its low roofline and ground-hugging stance gives it the look of a coupe.

The 3.5-liter (213 cid) V6 is standard. The 5.7-liter (348 cid) Hemi offers 340bhp, and in 6.1-liter (372 cid) SRT-8 trim there's 425bhp.

The 300 is rear-drive and gives a choice of fully automated or manual shifts. Loaded with electronic driver aids and a taut chassis, the 300 handles corners as well as the straights. The Chrysler 300 is here to stay.

Specification

Years built	1955 to 1963, 2003 to date
Most powerful model	2005 SRT-8
Engine type	V8
Displacement	372 cu in
Transmission	five-speed automatic
Power	425bhp
Top speed	150mph

1955 300 (above) and meeting 2005 SRT-8 (right)

2005 SRT-8
(above) and
1955 300-C
(left)

Dodge Challenger

It was a late challenge by Dodge but this car certainly made a big impact

The Challenger joined the muscle car market pretty late. With a lifespan of only five years, it really made its mark on the scene.

This Plymouth Barracuda-based model had a wide range of engines available when it first went on sale in 1970.

Performance versions, badged R/T (Road/Track) came as standard with a 335bhp 383 cid engine, with two optional 440 cid V8s available: the four-barrel Magnum with 375bhp

and the triple-carburated Six Pack with 390. Top dog was the awesome 426 Hemi with an outrageous 425bhp.

The 440s and Hemi came with TorqueFlite automatic transmission as standard, with a four-speed stick shift and limited slip differential both optional. The Charger even came in hardtop two-door or convertible body styles.

Dodge built a street version of its Trans Am racecar, the Challenger T/A, but when the

company's lack of success on the race track caused them to pull out after the 1970 series, they pulled the road car as well.

The Challenger's late start meant that it hit 1971's new, stricter US emissions laws in only its second year, and sales dropped off along with the power output of the engines. The Hemi retained its 425bhp rating and was still offered, but the 440 Six Pack was now reduced to 385bhp.

Its reputation was tarnished

MODEL HISTORY

1970
Challenger is launched with an impressive engine line-up including jaw-dropping 426 Hemi

1971
A Challenger pace car crashes into a press box at the Indy 500. The press are not impressed

1972
New grille fails to hid the fact that the Challenger is losing its muscle, with top power only 240bhp

1973
New 360 V8 only makes 5bhp more than the 340 that it replaces

1974
The Challenger bites the dust

even further when a
convertible, acting as pace
car for the Indy 500,
crashed very publicly into
the press box.

In 1972, the R/T
performance version was
discontinued and the
convertible version that
caused so much
embarassment at
Indianapolis in 1971 was
also dropped. Coincidence?

Now a 340 cid V8 with
just 240bhp was the biggest
engine on offer. Symbolic of
the Challenger's

Specification

Years built	1970 to 1975
Most powerful model	426 Hemi
Engine type	V8
Displacement	426 cu in
Transmission	TorqueFlite automatic
Power	425bhp
Top speed	140mph

emasculation was the R/T's
replacement, the new
Rallye edition, which
packed only a 318 cubic
inch V8 with just 150bhp.

When that was dropped
in '73, the only option for
for performance became
the new, 245bhp 360
engine – and it remained so
until Dodge admitted that
the Challenger had been
defeated in 1974.

Dodge *Charger*

Dodge's Mustang rival was late to the party, but Hemi power made it a legend that lives on today

The Dodge Charger was first shown to the public during the auto show season of 1965 as the Charger II concept car. It had a sleek two-door fastback body, hidden headlamps and full-width tail lamps. It had four bucket seats that further emphasized this car's performance potential. Within a year the production Charger was on sale, based on the Coronet, but looking almost identical to the show car, right down to those bucket seats.

Backing up that need for speed styling was a choice of V8 engines. Standard issue was a 318 cubic incher with 230bhp and next up was a 361 with 265bhp, but the most popular choice would prove to be the 383 with its 335bhp, giving its owners plenty of "bangs per buck".

For 1967 Dodge found a cheaper alternative for those demanding serious horsepower. In went the 440 Magnum engine as part of the Charger's R/T pack. But real performance fans could still choose the 426.

1968 saw the Charger's first major restyle with a new grille hiding the headlights, and a tweaked tail. The so-called Scat Pack added bumble bee stripes.

The big news for '69 came from the racing scene, with the NASCAR-derived Charger 500 and Daytona hitting the

1966 Original (opposite) and concepts from 1965 (above) and 1999 (below)

The most spectacular, however, was the 426 Street Hemi. Race-bred, but tuned for the road, this legendary engine had an official rating of 425bhp - but had closer to 500bhp. That gave the Charger the ability to run from zero to sixty in 6.4 seconds and do the standing quarter-mile in just 14 seconds. But the Hemi was expensive, adding $1,000 to the price tag and although Chargers were leaving Dodge dealerships quickly, few were Hemis.

MUSCLE CARS

MODEL HISTORY

1965
Charger II concept car unveiled

1966
Charger hits the streets with awesome Hemi engine as an option

1967
440 Magnum engine offered

1968
First major restyle

1969
Charger 500 and Daytona launched. The year of the General Lee

road and track. The regular Charger was pretty much unchanged from '68. It's probably the most famous, thanks to a starring role as The General Lee in the hit TV show The Dukes of Hazzard.

1970 brought a second facelift, including a bold chrome loop front bumper and new tail lights. Plum Crazy and Go-Mango were added to the colors, and the four-speed shifter now boasted a very cool pistol grip. In the engine bay there was a new option; the 440 Six Pack which ditched the standard four-barrel caburator in favour of three Holley two-barrel carbs. The result was a rise from 375bhp to 390bhp.

The early '70s brought doom and gloom. The restyled 1971 Charger now shared its body with the Dodge Super Bee and power outputs dropped, although not as much as rival muscle cars. However, Chrysler couldn't hold out for long and 1971 saw the end of the Hemi.

1973 arrived with another restyle. Hidden headlights vanished from the options list and the styling was softened. The suspension was, too, meaning the Charger was no longer a real street racer. For true fans the Charger died in 1974. But for 2006 Chrysler is reviving

the Charger name and the car's true spirit. 2006's Charger is more muscular, with a blunt snout and kicked up flanks. The high sides and low glass area give the Charger an almost coupe-like look, despite it actually having four doors. Charger purists have bemoaned the fact that beneath the styling, the new Charger is essentially the same as the Chrysler 300C.

But no enthusiast will have any gripes about the Charger's powerplant. Budget buyers can opt for a 3.5-liter (214 cid) High Output V6 engine with 250 horsepower, but it's the revived Hemi that will get Charger fans going.

The 5.7-liter (347 cid) Hemi packs a 340bhp punch and empowers the Charger with a zero to sixty time of just six seconds. Drive goes to the rear thanks to a five-speed automatic transmission with Chrysler's Autostick manual override system.

1999 concept car with ancestors (right),
2006 Charger Police spec (below)

THE ULTIMATE
CHARGER

Many will argue that a '68 Street Hemi should be king of the Chargers, but the fact is the latest 2006 SRT-8 would nail it in a straight line and around every corner. With its 425bhp Hemi engine it's got less raw power than a '68 but it weighs less too and is able to run from zero to sixty in five seconds and do the quarter-mile in 13 seconds. More impressively it can go from 0-100mph-0 in 16 seconds and stop from 60mph in just 110 feet. Special tuned SRT suspension is fitted alongside Brembo brakes and Goodyear F1 Supercar tires on 20-inch alloy wheels.

And as if that wasn't enough the SRT-8 version has an enlarged 6.1-liter (372 cid) Hemi with 425bhp.

But where the new Charger differs substantially is in its all-round performance ability. The original Charger would charge all right, but cornering and stopping weren't its favourite tasks. The 2006 Charger runs on 18-inch performance tires and tuned dampers and there's a Performance Handling Group option to give more steering feedback, better grip and enhanced roadholding. The SRT-8 also gets special Brembo brakes for added stopping power.

The new Charger, not quite the same as the original, is still every bit the 21st century muscle car.

Specification

Years built	1966 to 1978, 2005 to date
Most powerful model	2005 SRT-8
Engine type	V8
Displacement	372 cu in
Transmission	five-speed
Autostick	
Power	425bhp
Top speed	160mph

1969 Charger (above) and 968 Charger III concept (right)

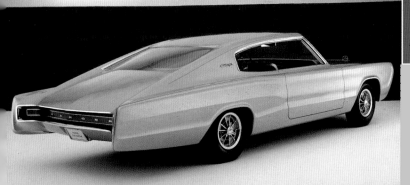

1968 model (above) and 1965 Charger II concept (left)

*2006 SRT-8
(above) and
1999 Charger
concept*

2006 R/T Chargers (above) and 2006 SRT-8 (left)

Dodge
Coronet

Packing a full race 426 Hemi V8, the Coronet was a mid-size with major muscle

Dodge used and then dropped the Coronet name back in the Fifties, but it returned in 1965.

This car meant business right from the start, being available with the awe-inspiring full race 426 Hemi. This race-bred V8, seriously under-rated at 425bhp, was a little too uncivilised for most and the following year saw the arrival of the Street Hemi.

Made more manageable by the fitting of a hydraulic lifter cam and a lower compression ratio, it still made the Coronet a fearsomely high performance car.

New for 1967 was the Coronet R/T, marketed as the model equally at home on road or track. It came with heavy-duty suspension and the standard power unit was a new Magnum 440 cid

MODEL HISTORY

1965
Coronet instantly stamps its mark on the muscle car scene, with full race 426 Hemi

1966
The Street Hemi is introduced – same engine but a slightly less raw state of tune

1967
Coronet R/T arrives, with standard Magnum 440, and the range is facelifted

1968
Full restyle introduces more rounded lines, but Charger and Super Bee steal Coronet's thunder

1970
Another facelift, but this is the final year of the high performance Coronets

V8, giving 375bhp when fitted with a four-barrel carburator and working through automatic or four-speed manual transmission. The Coronet range also received added racing stripes and deep front bucket seats.

A full restyle in 1968 resulted in more flowing, Coke-bottle-inspired lines, but internal competition from other Dodge performance models was

looming. The R/T badging was now shared with the more expensive, more alluring Charger and midway through the year

the company's new Super Bee undercut the Coronet on price.

The next year saw a new optional engine, the 440 Six Pack, created by fitting three two-barrel carbs to the existing 440 cid V8 and endowing it with 390bhp. A restyled front end in 1970 failed to attract further buyers and from 1971 on, the Coronet's days as a muscle car were over.

Specification

Years built	1965 to 1970
Most powerful model	1965 426 Hemi
Engine type	V8
Displacement	426 cu in
Transmission	four-speed manual
Power	425bhp
Top speed	130mph

Dodge
Daytona

Dodge's monster racecar for the road was the talk of 1969

Outrageous. That's the only way to describe the Dodge Daytona.

In 1969, the science of aerodynamics was at the cutting edge of race development, with the Ford's Torino Talladega and Mercury Cyclone Spoiler gaining supremacy. Dodge's engineers knew they could do better. They created a wild, 18-foot long supercar in the process.

They took the existing Charger 500 into surgery. The Daytona emerged from the wind tunnel with a drag coefficient of just 0.28 (compare that to the modern Dodge Viper's figure of 0.5!).

There would have been even less drag if it weren't for that huge rear wing, which helped to maintain traction on the rear at high

MODEL HISTORY

1969
Dodge Charger 500 racecar receives heavy aerodynamic restyle and the Daytona is born

1969
The company has to sell 500 road cars for the racecar to become eligible for NASCAR

1969
The car takes the first four places at Daytona, fulfilling Dodge's racing ambitions

1969
Sales of the street car fail to follow on from the racing success, with only 503 produced

1970
The Daytona doesn't make it into Dodge's road car brochure

speeds. A Daytona racecar hit the headlines with a world closed-course speed record of 201.14mph and another reached 217mph at the Bonneville salt flats.

For the racecar to be eligible for NASCAR, Dodge had to sell 500 Daytonas to the public, so the guy on the street had the chance to buy a hardcore track car that was road legal. The $4,000 price tag was high but not exorbitant, with the standard 440-engined

version offering a cheaper option with 375bhp. The fearsome 426 Hemi, with its race-bred 425bhp V8, was certainly not for the faint-hearted.

But the very thing that made it a winner on the track – its aerodynamic add-ons – proved a turn-off for the public. And so did its habit of overheating at speeds below 55mph!

Specification

Years built	1969
Most powerful model	1969 426 Hemi
Engine type	V8
Displacement	426 cu in
Transmission	four-speed manual
Power	425bhp
Top speed	160mph

Dodge
Super Bee

Dodge's answer to the Plymouth Road Runner never quite took off

The late Sixties saw the height of performance mania in the USA. With the effects of prosperity filtering down to the country's youth, virtually every 20-year-old with a job could afford an automobile.

This was an emerging market that astute car manufacturers were keen to tap into. It spurred Dodge, Plymouth's fellow Chrysler brand, to bring out its own vehicle for giving the kids cheap thrills – the Super Bee.

Released to the public later that same year, the Dodge also shared the same basic chassis, had a virtually identical curb weight. It was offered with the same range of engines as the Plymouth. But the Road Runner undercut the Super Bee's $3,027 base price by $131, putting the Dodge at a disadvantage from day one.

Still, at least the Super Bee looked the part. Bold bumble bee stripes circled the car's tail and it wore a big Super Bee

emblem proudly on its flanks.

Based on the redesigned Coronet pillared coupe, the Super Bee was offered with only two engines: the standard 335bhp 383 cubic inch V8 or the Chrysler group's prodigiously powerful 426 Hemi.

It may seem strange today, with original Hemi Super Bees hitting prices near to $100,000, but as this engine option added $1,000 to the price, the car's budget-conscious buyers tended to shy away from it.

MODEL HISTORY

1968	1969	1970	1970	1971
Super Bee introduced as a rival to Plymouth's successful Road Runner	*Two-door hardtop model joins the original pillared coupe*	*A restyle and a $64 drop in price fail to stop sales dropping*	*Wild colors like Plum Crazy and Go-Mango are offered*	*Super Bee adopts Dodge Charger platform, but the buzz is over*

The Bee's low purchase price was achieved by minimising equipment. Automatic transmission was an option from the standard four-speed manual shift, but if you wanted disc brakes, air conditioning or cruise control, the 1969 Dodge Super Bee couldn't deliver.

The same year saw the arrival of the Six Pack engine, as offered in the rest of Dodge's muscle car roster, giving buyers an optional 390bhp

Specification

Years built	1968 to 1971
Most powerful model	1968 426 Hemi
Engine type	V8
Displacement	426 cu in
Transmission	Four-speed manual
Power	425bhp
Top speed	125mph

powerplant topped off with a wild, air-scooped hood. Made of fiber glass it even had NASCAR-style tie-downs to complete the street racer look.

Despite 1970's eye-popping color schemes (such as Plum Crazy and Go-Mango) and a switch to the Dodge Charger platform in 1971, the model didn't make it into the 1972 sales season.

Dodge *Viper*

The Viper was a concept car made real and it turned round Dodge's fortunes in the 1990s

The Dodge Viper exploded onto the scene at the 1989 Detroit Auto Show and moved the muscle car into a whole new era. Big, brash and brawny, within three years the Viper was in the showrooms and an American dream was realised.

But it was harsh reality that helped create this dream car, which spearheaded an attempt by Chrysler to re-energize itself. The corporation was struggling in the late Eighties and its Vice President Bob Lutz was looking to produce a headline-grabbing sports car to put it back on the map. When

Carroll Shelby, the famous Texan ex-racer and creator of the legendary AC Cobra of the Sixties, joined the project he brought with him a burning desire to reproduce his success in building an iconic American performance car.

That was exactly what ended

2003 SRT-10 (left), first gen trio (above), 1989 concept (below)

rolled out of the showrooms, it was 1992. Chrysler was suddenly cool again.

Nothing could challenge the Viper's reign as the supreme expression of American automobile performance, and it remained basically unrivalled for nearly a decade. The introduction of the GTS coupe in 1996 provided a hardtop alternative to the R/T model's removable roof and featured an uprated 450bhp engine, but changed little else. The Viper was continuing to prove a popular image-booster but it needed an overhaul to maintain its profile.

up wowing the crowds at that Detroit Show – the spiritual descendant of the awesome Cobra. A raw, no-frills beast with monstrous power from a huge V10 engine, the Viper's vital statistics were: 488 cubic inches displacement, 400 horsepower and 465 lbft of torque. The bodywork was pure muscle, a strict two-seater layout fleshed out with beefy haunches and a huge hood to cover that aluminum-block V10 which promised 160mph performance.

By the time the first Vipers

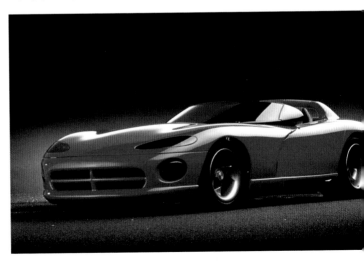

MUSCLE CARS

MODEL HISTORY

1989
The Viper concept car makes its first public appearance, wowing the Detroit Auto Show

1989
A wave of positive feedback convinces Chrysler bosses to put it into production

1992
First R/T model cars are delivered to buyers. Only 285 are made – all in red

1996
GTS fixed-head coupe version launched with an uprated 450bhp engine

1996
RT/10 upped to 415bhp when side-exit exhausts are replaced by a rear-exit system

When Dodge engineers literally tried to change the car's profile by adding a few inches to the wheelbase, they discovered that they would also need to rework most of the body panels and suspension. So they decided they may as well create an entirely new car: a true convertible with a revised chassis and shell... and an even bigger, more powerful engine!

Dodge realised the passion that the Viper stirred in its owners and asked them for feedback on what they would like. The feedback was resounding: they wanted more power, less weight, bigger brakes and no unnecessary add-ons like cruise control or cupholders. In a true power-to-the-people gesture, Dodge set to its task...

When the new 2003 Viper SRT-10 emerged, it performed pretty much to the brief these owners had given. It was 100 pounds lighter than the outgoing model. The car still packed a V10 under the hood, but the new engine displaced 505 cubic inches, producing 500 horsepower and a massive 525 lbft of torque. The previous model's six-speed manual transmission was beefed up. A stiffer chassis held everything together, with revised suspension.

The new suspension improved ride quality and the brakes received

1997

RT/10 receives
the uprated
450bhp engine

1998

GT2 prod
limited n
100 to cel
success in
racing

attention too, with improved Brembo calipers which Dodge claimed would haul the car to a stop from 60mph in an impressive 100 feet. The remainder of the SRT-10's performance statisics are equally staggering: 0-60mph in less than four seconds, a top speed of 190mph and 0-100-0mph in less than 13 seconds.

In addition, the SRT-10's colossal rear wheels were the widest available on a stock US production car, at 19x13 inches – and the fronts were no slouches at 18x10. The huge contact area of the tires combined with the car's longer wheelbase made the big snake less unpredictable when really pushed.

The general refinements in the Viper's driving experience were echoed with appointments which made living with a Viper a little less rough and ready. The car was now a true convertible. Gone was the R/T's clumsy

Latest SRT-10 on the road (below and right)

THE ULTIMATE
VIPER

The snake car continues to evolve, and the next expression of the Viper's extreme performance philosophy is the 2006 SRT-10 Coupe. The ultimate Viper, this car is based on the SRT-10 convertible, but with a fixed metal roof featuring 'double bubble' bulges to give more headroom for driver and passenger. That's to allow the wearing of crash helmets – so there's absolutely no doubt about this car's sporting intent! The 2006 Coupe's engine and drivetrain are shared with the convertible, so there's still 505 cubic inches of displacement, 500 horsepower and 525 lb-ft of torque driving through a six-speed manual transmission. But as the coupe is more aerodynamic than the convertible, it will beat the latter's 190mph top speed.

removable roof. Now it had an easily-operated bi-fold clamshell top that stowed neatly under the trunk lid. Although still recognizably a Viper, the new model's bodywork was sleeker if a little less muscular than its predecessor. The new conventionally-hinged hood was certainly easier to handle than the old

front-hinged job. But some Viper fans mourned the passing of the 'cartoon muscle car' looks of the original.

Now well into its second decade, the Viper continues to provide the glamour that it first injected into the company back in 1992. Its reliability and longevity has been backed up by repeated success in endurance racing.

Specification

Years built	1992 to date
Most powerful model	2005 SRT-10
Engine type	V10
Displacement	505 cu in
Transmission	six-speed manual, rear-wheel drive
Power	500bhp
Top speed	190mph

1997 R/T-10 (above) and an early '92 (right)

2003 SRT-10
(above) and ear
R/T-10 (left)

2003 SRT-10 (above) and alongside 2006 Coupe (right)

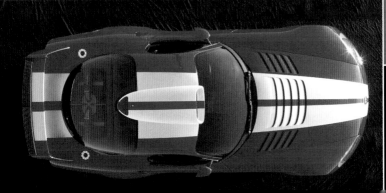

2006 Coupe
(above) and the
concept that
spawned it (left)

Ford *Fairlane*
& *Torino*

The Fairlane was a real innovator, but it also had plenty of muscle.
And as a Gran Torino it became one of the most popular TV cars ever

Probably one of the few cars to be named after a house – Henry Ford's Fair Lane mansion in Dearborn – this fairly ordinary family sedan evolved into a

range of remarkable autos over 16 years from1955.

The 1957 'Skyliner' had the world's first fully retractable electrically-powered steel roof.

The sleek 1960 'Starliner', a pillarless two-door hardtop, set the much-copied 'fastback' look. The 1962 Fairlane 500 Sports Coupe had bucket seats and an

Sports Coupe was nearly a foot shorter than the previous year's car and boasted a new lightweight 'thin-wall-cast' 221 cubic inch V8. It even had European sports car style bucket seats.

The most muscular Fairlane ever has to be the 1964 Thunderbolt or 'T-Bolt'. Specially built for drag strip racing, the cars' big 427 cubic inch V8s were rated at 425 horsepower, but actually produced 500. In the 1964 NHRA's World Championship, a T-Bolt driven by Gas Ronda took 1st place. Just 111 T-Bolts were built.

1967 Fairlane (opposite page), 1969 Torino (above) and 1969 convertible (right)

innovative lightweight thin-wall cast V8. The 1964 427 cubic inch Fairlane 'Thunderbolt' or 'T-Bolt', built specially for serious drag-strip racing, boasted a highly tuned 427 cubic inch V8 with an astonishing 500 bhp. Fairlane spin-offs, included the mighty Galaxie, the Fairlane GT and GTA, the 500 XL GT hardtop and convertible, and 'Zebra Three'.

The Fairlane didn't enter the ranks of the muscle cars until the middle of 1962. The Fairlane 500

MUSCLE CARS

In 1966, Ford added the Fairlane GT and GTA 500 XL cars. These were fitted with Ford's big-block FE V8 and had special badges, body stripes, heavy duty suspension, disc brakes, bucket seats, and sports steering wheel. The XL featured a 390 cubic inch 335 horsepower V8 with a high-lift cam, performance manifolds and a four-barrel carb. To improve its muscle-car image Ford also made around 60 Fairlanes fitted with the famous 'side-oiler' 427 wedge engines that were raced in NASCAR.

In 1968 the famous Torino was introduced, its most powerful version a 390bhp 427 cubic inch V8. In 1969, the Torino Cobra was added with lowered and toughened suspension, wide wheels, black grille and hood air-scoop. Its 428 cubic inch Cobra Jet V8 was rated at 335bhp, but it really cranked out 400.

1975 was the year of the Torino and the screening of Starsky and Hutch, whose stars thundered around in a red and white Gran Torino call-signed 'Zebra Three'. The car became so popular that Ford reacted by making 1,000 look-alikes.

Specification

Years built	1955 to 1971
Most powerful model	1969 Fairlane Cobra
Engine type	V8
Displacement	428 cu in
Transmission	four-speed manual
Power	335bhp
Top speed	125mph

MODEL HISTORY

1955
Ford Fairlane launched as a top of the line full-size Ford in six different body styles

1957
Fairlane 500 Skyliner is the first in the world with an electric retractable hardtop

1960
The Fairlane 'Starliner', a pillarless two-door hardtop, set the much-copied 'fastback' look

1962
First of the Fairlane muscle-cars. Fairlane 500 Sports Coupe

1964
Thunderbolt drag-strip racer is most powerful version of the Fairlane with up to 500bhp

Ford *Galaxie*

It was the most powerful muscle car ever made, but the Galaxie's performance didn't translate into sales

The Galaxie has the distinction of having the most powerful engine of the muscle-car era. The Cammer 427 engine was developed for the 1965 car and in its dual-four-barrel carb form was rated at a colossal 675bhp. It was, and probably still is, the most powerful production engine ever made in Detroit. However, it made the Galaxie almost impossible to drive on the street. Too few cars were fitted with it for NASCAR to accept the Cammer as a production engine and Ford stopped production.

The first Galaxie was launched in 1959 and came with Ford's first production muscle-car engine, the 352 Interceptor Special V8. Rated at 360bhp, it had a four-barrel carb, 10.6:1 compression, a solid-lifter cam and a dual-point distributor.

V8. With a single four-barrel Holly carb, it was rated at 385bhp, and with three Holley dual-barrel carbs it put out 405bhp. Even then it was down four horses on Chevrolet's 409bhp 409 cubic inch V8. The 406 engine was a must to get the big and heavy Galaxies moving in a respectable fashion.

In 1962, the 406 engine was made available in the lighter Galaxie 500 and 500 XL. The XL had bucket seats and a center console. Both of these 'sportier' Galaxies came with floor-stick four-speed manual transmission, 15-inch

1969 convertible (above) and 1969 XL (opposite page and right)

In 1960, Ford withdrew from the Auto Manufacturers Association's four year ban on stock car racing and almost immediately turned up at the Daytona Speedway with a 360bhp Galaxie Starliner. The 1961 Starliner was smaller in size but much bigger-engined. In the middle of the year the 390 cubic inch V8 was available with a triple two-barrel carb rated at a massive 401 horsepower. It reached 60 miles an hour in just seven seconds.

Cubic inches counted in the early 60s and Ford came up with the 406 cubic inch

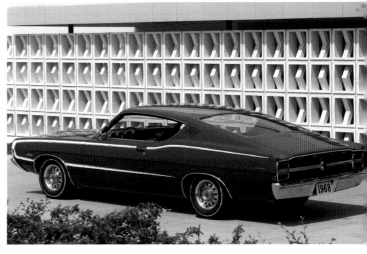

MUSCLE CARS

instead of 14-inch wheels and heavy-duty suspension.

1963 turned out to be a good year for the Galaxie. The two-door hardtop was re-styled and lowered to improve aerodynamics, and with the new 427 cubic inch 425bhp motor, it won no less than 23 Grand National NASCAR races – including the top five places at Daytona.

Ford also built 50 lightweight Sports Roof Galaxies specially for competition. And with the 425bhp 427 engine the lightweights could manage the quarter-mile in a respectable 12.07 seconds.

1965 saw the Cammer 427, the most powerful production engine ever made in Detroit. With a single barrel carb, this twin-overhead camshaft was rated at a colossal 616bhp. With dual four-barrel carbs the power output was a hardly believable 675bhp. The 'cammer' Galaxie was impossible to drive on the street and NASCAR didn't accept it. Unfortunately only 237 427-engined cars were sold in 1966, signalling the end of the Galaxie's heydays as a muscle car. From 1967 until its demise in 1972, the Galaxie was developed and promoted as a limo.

Specification

Years built	1969 to 1972
Most powerful model	1965 Cammer
Engine type	V8
Displacement	427 cu in
Transmission	four-speed manual
Power	675bhp
Top speed	130mph

MODEL HISTORY

1959
Galaxie launched with Ford's first production muscle-car engine, the 352 Interceptor Special

1960
Galaxie Starliner does 40 laps at Daytona at an average speed of 142mph

1961
406 cubic inch V8 introduced. With three Holley dual-barrel carbs it puts out 405bhp

1962
Galaxie 500 and 500 XL introduced. Both come with floor-stick four-speed manual transmission

1963
Galaxie wins 23 Grand National NASCAR races – including the top five places at Daytona

1964

Lightweight
Sports Roof
Galaxies run the
quarter-mile in
12.07 seconds

1965

Introduction of
Detroit's most
powerful production
engine ever – the
675bhp Cammer

1966

427-engined
Galaxie sales drop
away with just
237 cars sold

1967

Galaxie muscle car
image dropped as
car is promoted as
luxury limousine

1972

Galaxie production
ends. Top of the
line limo is the
spacious LTD
Brougham

Ford *GT*

*To celebrate its 100th anniversary Ford recreated
a racing legend with the glorious GT*

The tale of Ford's amazing GT40 is the story of an American company's burning desire to win the world's toughest endurance race against all the odds. Four decades after the original events, the rebirth of a legend in the form of the awesome Ford GT has occurred.

Back in the early Sixties Ford set itself the task of winning the prestigious Le Mans 24 Hour race. By taking the honours the corporation hoped to increase sales of its road cars.

In an attempt to fast-track his company to sporting glory, Ford boss Henry Ford II tried to buy Ferrari, the Italian company which had made Le Mans its own with six consecutive victories. Rebuffed

A place in sportscar history was sealed and it seemed that the GT40's influence would be limited to being one of the most popular shapes on the kit car scene. A detuned roadgoing version of the car was offered from 1967. But few were sold and the rarity of these automobiles added to the model's mystique.

The rebirth of Ford's legend was heralded by a modern interpretation of the GT40, a concept car shown at the Detroit Auto Show of 2003. The show car proved a massive hit and precipitated the decision to produce a road-legal

Le Mans 1,2,3 of 1966 (above) and 2004's tire fryer (below)

by the firm's owner, Enzo Ferrari, Ford determined to produce, from scratch, a sportscar to crush the Italians on the track.

On a tight schedule, work started in 1963, with the first prototype produced early in '64. After two failed attempts, the 1966 Le Mans 24 Hours with Ford's GT40s coming first, second and third. In three short years, the company had made Henry Ford II's impossible dream come true – and the GT40 went on to an unbroken string of Le Mans wins from 1966-69.

production model.

Just like its spiritual successor, the new car, would need to be ready in just 16 months. Considering that it was to be a re-interpretation of a classic racecar, it was a tall order.

The GT40 formula – a hugely powerful American V8, mid-mounted just behind the driver, clothed in low-slung racecar bodywork – was given a 21st century treatment. But this was to be a road car, so the original's 40-inch roof height (which famously helped to coin its name) would have to be stretched. In fact, the cabin's overall dimensions were enlarged.

Using the latest computerized design technology, Ford designers and engineers labored to create a modern supercar to evoke the spirit of the Sixties legend. The machine they produced reflected its heritage perfectly, its sleek silouhette echoing the GT40's attitude despite completely different dimensions.

At the heart of the GT is that mid-mounted 330 cubic-inch V8 which sends 550 horsepower and 500lbft to the rear wheels. This high-tech, supercharged example of the engine-builder's art drives through a six-speed manual transmission, putting an indomitable surge of urge at the driver's disposal.

The GT is breathtakingly fast.

THE ULTIMATE
FORD GT

The most successful GT40 ever is the car which won Le Mans in 1968 and '69 – chassis number GT40P/1075. Built in '68, this was one of the Gulf Racing cars finished in the team's famous powder blue and orange racing colours. With a super-light and incredibly strong aluminium-honeycomb shell, this ultimate development of the race car was capable of a 220mph top speed. When it comes to who's the daddy of all GTs, it's easy – they all are. Ford only offers this modern-day supercar in one version. Guess they think that just owning one of these cars is the ultimate in itself!

A test driver for the American automobile magazine Car and Driver in 2004 managed a 0-60mph blast in a stupendous 3.3 seconds and recorded a scorching quarter-mile time of 11.6 seconds at 128mph. Pitted against Ferrari's Challenge Stradale and Porsche's 911 GT3, the Ford wiped the floor with its opponents, the Ferrari only managing four seconds to 60mph and being 0.8secs and 13mph slower through the quarter mile. Ford GT showed the Italians the way once more!

Despite the monstrous power, the GT is an easy car to drive. The power-assisted steering, clutch pedal and stick shift are light to operate, with the brake pedal giving access to the astounding decelerative effects of huge Brembo rotors.

With an aluminum spaceframe and body panels, a fiberglass hood and with carbon-

2004 trio (below), and GT at 205mph (right)

fiber used in the underbody aerodynamic system and the seats, modern weight-saving methods are much in evidence. And the modern attitude to comfort is also displayed in this car's interior. The GT's doors are deep cut into the roof, echoing the originals, and after hitting the red starter button, you can see the supercharger doing its thing as you sit in the driver's seat.

Nobody knows how long the Ford GT will stay in production. The intention was always that this "Pace car for a whole company" would be produced in limited numbers, with Ford aiming to build around 1,500 a year until demand tailed off. This is one exclusive vehicle, with a selling price of $140,000.

Specification

Years built	2004 to date
Most powerful model	2004 GT
Engine type	supercharged V8
Displacement	330 cu in
Transmission	six-speed manual, rear-wheel drive
Power	550bhp
Top speed	205mph

Ford GTs on track in 2004 (above) and 1966 (right)

2004 GT opens *
in the garage (ab
and on the road

2004 GT glamor (above and right)

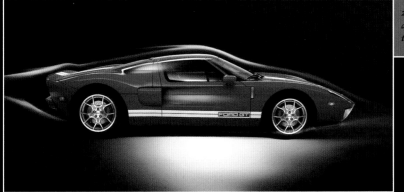

2004 GTs (above) and in wind tunnel (left)

Ford *Mustang*

*The original Pony Car has also proved the
most successful over the last forty years*

It was April 1964, mid-size muscle cars were hot, but Ford boss Lee Iacocca thought the public was ready for something else; a small, light and inexpensive sports car. The Ford Mustang.

Originally conceived as a two-seater, Iacocca realized that selling the car in big numbers meant it needed to be more practical. So the Mustang that made its debut at the 1964 World's Fair in New York was shown as a four-seater convertible and hardtop. It was a huge hit, with 22,000 orders received on the first day and one million Mustangs sold within the first two years. The Mustang was a phenomenon, despite not offering anything like the power of true muscle cars. At launch the Mustang came with a 170

the back seat, the Shelby Mustang would become a legend in its own right.

To make the Mustang affordable Ford had based it on the Falcon, and by 1966 it was decided to hide its roots with an all-new instrument pack. The 260 was dropped and two versions of the 289 offered instead. The Shelby GT-350 could now be specified with an automatic transmission and Hertz rent-a-car even bought a number to rent to weekend racers.

1967 brought the Mustang's first major restyle. It was a heavier look, but

1964 convertible (opposite page), 1967 GT 500 (above) and 1973 Mach 1 (right)

cubic inch straight-six with just 101bhp. Ford quickly realised that this wasn't enough and by the middle of 1964 a 289 K-code V8 was offered with a much more appetising 271bhp as standard as well as a 165bhp 260.

A fastback also arrived and with it a tie-up with racing legend Carroll Shelby. The Shelby GT-350 came with 306bhp in street specification, but the race-ready 350R weighed in with 360bhp. Stripped of any excess weight, including

MUSCLE CARS

MODEL HISTORY

1964
Mustang launched at World's Fair. 22,000 orders on the first day

1964
The first Shelby Mustang GT350 appears

1967
Mustang restyled, Shelby GT500 introduced

1968
Cobra Jet engine fitted, with up to 410bhp

1969
Mustang Mach 1 fastback goes on sale

more muscular, to compete with the likes of the Chevrolet Camaro SS. A 390 big block V8 was dropped in, although the GT350 still used the 289. Shelby raised his game with the GT500, powered by a race-bred 427 packing 355bhp.

In 1968 the Mustang received the legendary 428 Cobra Jet engine. With ram air induction it produced 335bhp although everyone knew that it was really more like 410bhp. Top of the heap was the GT500KR – King of the Road – with its Cobra Jet engine and Shelby's magic worked on it.

1969's second restyle introduced the Mach 1 fastback body and saw the first Boss cars. With race-ready V8s in 302 or 429 cubic inch capacity the Boss cars were basically NASCAR racers for the road and the 429 offered a mighty 375bhp.

Sadly, 1970 saw the demise of the Shelby Cobra and by 1971 the Mustang's days as a muscle car were numbered.

1974's second generation was supposed to retrace the car's original roots as a small lightweight sports car. But the Mustang II was underpowered, too heavy and the performance was pitiful. The top flight 2.8-liter V6 took nearly 14 seconds to reach 60mph.

1974
Mustang II unveiled, but is a slow performer and a slow seller

1974
Third generation Mustang starts to claw back lost ground

1994
30 years old and the Mustang's fourth generation arrives

2004
40th anniversary and the fifth generation Mustang arrives to celebrate

2005
Most powerful Mustang ever is launched. The Shelby Cobra GT500 has 450bhp

THE ULTIMATE MUSTANG

The 2005 Shelby Cobra GT500 is the most powerful Ford Mustang ever. With 450bhp from its 5.4-liter (305 cid) supercharged V8 engine it offers spectacular tire frying performance. Ford's Special Vehicle Team was employed to fine-tune the all-round independent suspension to give this car track-ready handling. 14-inch crossed drilled disc brakes provide awesome stopping power and the car is finished off with Shelby's trademark white racing stripes. It really is the ultimate Mustang.

The all-new Mustang of 1979 started to regain a little ground. The car was lighter and the most powerful turbocharged four-cylinder engine (still only 143bhp) gave a reasonable turn of speed. In '84 the Mustang celebrated 20 years with a 2.3-liter (140 cid) 174 bhp turbo engine or a five-liter V8 (305 cid) with a little less go and by the end of the Eighties the V8's power was upped to over 200bhp.

The fourth generation pony car came in 1994 with 3.8-liter (232 cid) V6 or five-liter (305 cid) V8 power. The restyle was softer than before but performance was gradually hardened up over its lifetime. It reached its peak in 2000 with the limited edition SVT Cobra R.

The latest Mustang arrived to celebrate the model's 40th anniversary.

2005 convertible (right) and 1996 Mustang GT (below)

A five-speed manual transmission is standard, with a five-speed automatic on the options list. There's independent suspension all-round, making this the finest handling Mustang ever. Powerful all-wheel disc brakes with ABS come as standard and there's a long list of electronic driver aids as well.

Finally, to bring this great legend up to date Ford announced the return of the Shelby GT500 in 2005. The Ford Shelby Cobra GT500 adds a supercharger to its 5.4-liter (329 cid)V8 engine to pump out more than 450bhp. Shelby's famous white racing stripes add the final touch. With millions sold, the Mustang is the ultimate muscle car success story.

Specification

Years built	1964 to date
Most powerful model	2005 Shelby Cobra
Engine type	V8
Displacement	329 cu in
Transmission	six-speed manual, rear-wheel drive
Power	450bhp
Top speed	160mph

1968 Shelby GT 500 convertible (above) and 1969 Shelby GT350 (right)

1982 Mustang 5.0 (above) and 1993 convertible (left)

2000 SVT Cobra (above) and 2005 convertible (right),

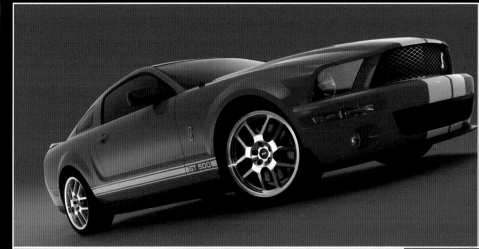

2005 Shelby Cobra GT500 (above) and with original (left)

Ford Thunderbird

Now celebrating 50 glorious years, the Ford Thunderbird has been a muscle car and a luxury car, but it's always been special

The name was inspired, the look low, long and stylish, and it was a hit from the word go in 1955.

Named after the great Thunderbird of Native American legend, Ford's first two-seater sports car was intended to compete with Chevrolet's

Corvette, but its eye-candy looks and high equipment levels created an entirely new market segment – the luxury personal sports car. There were 3,500 orders in the first ten days. And in keeping with the new concept the majority of the early

Thunderbirds left the dealers equipped with auto transmission and the 212 horsepower version of the 292 cubic inch V8.

The 1956 design changes included flip-out side vents for better ventilation, porthole windows in the removable

better handling and increased performance.

The E-code 312 V8 featured two four-barrel carbs and was rated at 270 bhp. The F-code 312 V8 featured a single four-barrel carb force fed by a Paxton-built McCulloch centrifugal supercharger. The F-code engine was rated at 300 bhp, or at 340 bhp with the optional NASCAR "racing kit." It would be the last of the two-seaters.

From 1958 until 1983, Ford built a heavier, more luxurious four-seater. The four-seat Thunderbird continued to be

2005 convertible (opposite page), 1957 (above) and 1962 (below)

hardtop, improved rear quarter vision and an outside tire carrier added trunk space.

Ford also introduced its new safety idea of "packaging the passengers". Standard safety equipment included energy-absorbing instrument panel padding, a concave safety steering wheel and a shatter-resistant mirror. Safety belts were optional.

Last-minute improvements, including the addition of the optional 312 cid V8 215 horsepower engine, gave the second edition of the Thunderbird

produced through the 80s and 90s, but the public taste for the car slowly declined, and Ford announced that the 1997 model would be the last in the line.

But the Thunderbird story doesn't end there. In 1999 a two-seater concept Thunderbird was revealed at the Detroit Auto Show. The concept car was a design exercise intended to gauge consumer reaction. It worked.

The car proved to be wildly popular with show-goers. Two years later, Ford announced Thunderbird's return.

The 2002 Thunderbird came to market in the summer of 2001 as a limited production model aimed at 20-25,000 units of annual production. It won critical acclaim for its modern interpretation of the classic original roadster styling and was

named Motor Trend's "Car of the Year."

A year on and the Thunderbird received improvements including an upgraded 280-horsepower V8. And in 2005, Ford marked the 50th anniversary of the Thunderbird with a special edition. It may not quite be the muscle car it once was, but the Thunderbird is as distinctive now as it was five decades ago.

Specification

Years built	1955 to date
Most powerful model	1957 F-code
Engine type	V8
Displacement	312 cu in
Transmission	three-speed automatic
Power	340bhp
Top speed	125mph

MODEL HISTORY

1955
Launch of Thunderbird, Ford's first two-seater sports car

1956
First restyle also brings option of 312 cubic inch V8 rated at 215 horsepower

1957
Last but most muscular and stylish of the two-seater Thunderbirds is built

1962
Sports Roadster launched with fiberglass tonneau that converts four-seater back into a two-seater

1971
Nieman-Marcus offer 'His and Her' Thunderbirds equipped with telephones and tape players

1975	1983	1999	2001	2005
Thunderbird weighs 5,000 pounds and sold as 'the epitome	*Introduction of the 'aero-style' Thunderbird*	*Thunderbird show car wows the crowds at Detroit Auto Show*	*New two-seat Thunderbird is Motor Trend Magazine's Car*	*Thunderbird celebrates 50 glorious years*

1965 Thunderbird (above) and 1972 (right)

2005
Thunderbird
celebrates 50
years (above
and left)

Mercury *Cougar*

*The Mustang-based Cougar came in with
a roar but went out with a whimper*

It may have the name of a wildcat but the Motor Trend 1967 Car of the Year Mercury Cougar was still classed as a pony car. It had the look of all the Mustang derivatives with a long front end and short rear deck, but the two-door hardtop Cougar looked a bit more balanced than the Mustang as it was three inches longer.

Its equipment also took it upmarket. The XR-7 and GT came with a wood-rimmed steering wheel and bucket seats, and the GT took the Cougar into the muscle car league with its 390 cubic inch 335bhp V8. The GT included firmer suspension, with stiffer springs and shocks, and power front disc brakes. The 390 engine had hydraulic valve lifters

1969 Eliminator (opposite page and below) and 1968 hardtop (above)

made it easier to meet increasingly stringent exhaust emission regulations.

1968 also saw the introduction of the Cougar XR-7G. The 'G' stood for Gurney – stock car race ace Dan Gurney who drove a Mercury briefly in 1968. In spite of its go-faster looks, in reality the car was no faster than the GT-E. Curiously the 'G' package was available with any Cougar. The add-ons included a fiberglass hood scoop, a racing mirror, an optional sunroof, spoke pattern wheels, four-pipe exhaust and special 'G' emblem badges. Not many 'G' Cougars were

and a four-barrel Holley carb.

The Cougar GT-E was new for 1968 and signalled an increase in performance with a 390bhp 427 cubic inch V8. But this engine made the car nose-heavy and it suffered from a distinct lack of grip off the line. Insurance company complaints led to this engine being replaced with the new and lighter Ford 428 cubic inch engine rated at a low 335bhp. But, according to many experts at the time, the actual output was closer to the 390 horses of the 427. The 428 had a longer piston stroke than the 427 which

MUSCLE CARS

made, so very few exist today.

Real performance was added to the Cougar in the middle of 1969 with the addition of the aggressively named Cougar 'Eliminator'. Although the 1969 Cougars were longer, wider and somewhat heavier the availability of the 428 Cobra Jet with Ram Air got the Cougar, with its longer wheelbase, quicker off the line than the Mustang –

though the quarter-mile mile times were about the same. With a black grille, front and rear spoilers, side stripes and day-glow blue, orange and yellow body colors, the Eliminators looked the business. The 335bhp 428 also got the Eliminator off the line to 60mph in 5.6 seconds and ran the quarter-mile in 14.1.

Mercury certainly reckoned thatbigger was better for the

Cougar in 1970. It also had a new look that further reflected its Mustang origins. The Eliminator stayed in the line-up and came with a 429 V8 with Ram-Air and a rated output of 375bhp.

Sales of the performance Cougars declined. The 429 cubic inch V8 was still on offer, but would be dropped for 1972.

Specification

Years built	1967 to 1973
Most powerful model	1970 Eliminator
Engine type	V8
Displacement	427 cu in
Transmission	three-speed automatic
Power	375bhp
Top speed	127mph

MODEL HISTORY

1967
Cougar is Motor Trend's Car of the Year

1967
Cougar GT has 390 cubic inch 335bhp V8

1968
Cougar GT-E launched with 390 bhp 427 cubic inch V8

1968
Dan Gurney inspired XR7-G fails to inspire many sales

1969
Stringent emission regulations lead to long-stroke 428

1969

Cougar 'Eliminator'
launched with
335bhp long-stroke
428 Ram Air
Cobra Jet V8

1969

Eliminator runs
the quarter-mile
in 14.1 seconds

1970

Eliminator scores
with 375bhp 429
cubic inch V8
with Ram-Air
induction

1971

Luxury pushed
instead of
performance as
sales of Cougar
decline

1972

Last of the
Cougar pony cars
as output drops
to 266 bhp

Mercury Cyclone

The warmed up Comet was a rival to the budget-priced Road Runner

The Mercury Cyclone was the hot version of the Mercury Comet. First announced in January 1964, its sporty features included bucket seats, an instrument console, chrome trim bits for the 210bhp 289 cubic inch V8, and chrome wheel trims that gave the impression – from a distance – that the car had chrome wheels. The Cyclone was a budget performer, but it was a performer nonetheless.

For 1966 the Comet was based on the larger Ford Fairlane. The wheelbase was now 116 inches and the front track was wider, making room

for Ford's big block engines.

Both hardtop and convertible body styles were available. There was also a GT option that included Ford's new 335bhp 390 cubic inch V8. Buyers could have a fibreglass hood with a fake scoop and GT stripes and badges. The standard transmission was a three-speed manual, with options of a four-speed manual or three-speed automatic.

The Cyclone and Cyclone GT continued in 1967, although for some reason the 390 cubic inch engine was downrated at 320bhp. The 1968 car had a facelift and a

new fastback coupe body style was added.

This was a wise move. The fastback outsold the notchback by a factor of 20 to one. The convertible was dropped. The most powerful engine of 1968 was the 390bhp 427 cubic inch V8. This was dropped after just a few months and replaced with Ford's legendary 428 Cobra Jet V8, with 335bhp.

1969 saw the introduction of the Cyclone CJ (Cobra Jet), aimed directly at the Plymouth Roda Runner in the low-price performance car market. The CJ standard engine was the 335bhp

MODEL HISTORY

1964
Mercury Cyclone introduced as sporty derivative of the Comet

1966
Cyclone based on larger Ford Fairlane makes room for big block engines

1967
New fastback body-style outsells notchback by 20 to one

1969
Cyclone CJ introduced – aimed at low-price performance car market

1972
Production of Mercury Comets and Comet Cyclones ends

428 cubic inch. The CJ also came with a four-speed manual transmission, a competition handling pack – and a bench seat.

The hottest Cyclone of the year was the Spoiler II with improved aerodynamics aimed at success on the NASCAR circuit. Spoilers came in two levels of trim, named after NASCAR heroes Dan Gurney (blue roof and stripes) and Cale Yarborough (red roof and stripes). Both came with a 351 four-barrell V8 not, as many hoped, the Cobra Jet. Sales of just 519 units hardly seemed worth the effort.

Further hot but re-styled and larger Cyclones continued through 1970, inlcuding a handful of BOSS 429-powered cars, but were dropped in 1971 as the muscle car era slowly came to an end. The last Cyclones were made in 1972.

Specification

Years built	1964 to 1972
Most powerful model	1969 CJ
Engine type	V8
Displacement	427 cid
Transmission	four-speed manual
Power	390bhp
Top speed	127mph

Oldsmobile
442

Oldsomobile's answer to the Pontiac GTO may not have been the first or coolest muscle car but it was the real deal

The 442 was originally a performance package rather than an actual model. The numbers signified a four-barrel carburator (4), a four-speed manual transmission (4) and dual exhausts (2), with these sporty ingredients offered on Oldsmobile's Cutlass. The recipe for the 442 was to change over the years, but the name stuck and was to become the byword for Olds' muscle cars.

The Cutlass 442 was launched after the Pontiac GTO had paved the way. Oldsmobile whacked its biggest-hitting power unit into its midsized chassis. At 330 cubic inches, this V8 came modified with all the performance equipment specified by police departments for pursuit cars. The deal also included heavy duty

442 emerged with a new option – the first opportunity to have triple carburretors fuelling the engine. The set-up was smooth and lifted power output to 360bhp, while suspension upgrades increased handling standards even further.

The tri-carb option didn't last long, with a GM ban on such set-ups forcing Oldsmobile to seek alternative methods to maintain power output in 1967. They did it with the W-30 package, a "forced air induction system" with special air ducting, plus an uprated camshaft and springs.

Awesome Olds/Hurst (opposite), 442 convertible (above) and coupe (right)

shocks and springs plus a rear stabilizer bar.

For 1965, Oldsmobile got its act together with its advertising, which gave the 442 a more youthful image and greater sales success. The performance package was more attractive too, with a new 400 cid V8 replacing the old unit, bringing power up to 345bhp. The new 442 pack also improved on the class-leading handling, with heavy duty shocks and springs, plus front and rear stabilizer bars along with fat tires.

Clothed in fresh sheet metal, the 1966 model Cutlass

MUSCLE CARS

The 442 of 1968 saw the famous name finally became a model designation in its own right. '68's biggest news was the Hurst/Olds. Originally a one-off marrying of the 442 with the 390 horsepower 455 cid V8 from Oldsmobile's Toronado, a limited run was sanctioned by the company. Capable of 0-60mph in 5.4 seconds, only 515 were made in '68, making them prized collector's items today. The Hurst/Olds returned for 1968, with a new colour scheme and extravagant bonnet scoops, although it was slightly detuned to 380bhp.

In 1970 GM's ban on engines over 400 cubic inches in midsized cars was lifted, allowing Oldsmobile to offer its 455 cid V8 in all 442s as standard. The Hurst/Olds was now dropped, not to reappear until 1972. The W-30 achieved its highest ever power output, thanks to a balanced, blueprinted and generally hotted-up version of the 455 V8. 1970 also saw the arrival of a new option, the Rallye 350 – its 310 horsepower engine wasn't exceptional, but the exterior treatment was, with bright yellow paint – even on the bumpers and wheels!

Specification

Years built	1964 to 1973
Most powerful model	1968 Hurst/Olds
Engine type	V8
Displacement	455 cu in
Transmission	four-speed manual, rear-wheel drive
Power	390bhp
Top speed	130mph

MODEL HISTORY

1964
442 option first offered on Oldsmobile's Cutlass model, with 310bhp, 330 cid V8

1965
New 400 cid, engine joins 442 package, generating increased power at 345bhp

1966
Tri-carb option gives 360bhp. 442's reputation for handling enhanced with suspension upgrade

1968
442 becomes a stand-alone model name. Top-dog Hurst/Olds introduced with 390bhp

1970
GM lifts ban on engines over 400 cid

Oldsmobile
Toronado

A front-drive muscle car? Nobody would have believed it until the Toronado

The Toronado was a truly radical machine. Never mind the amazing styling, the Toronado was the first and only true front-wheel drive muscle car.

The story started in 1966 when Oldsmobile launched the largest front-wheel drive car ever made. It received a fantastic reception from press and the public. Motor Trend magazine named the Toronado their Car of the Year.

With a wheelbase of 119 inches this was one big beast,

and at 4,366 pounds it was no lightweight, but Olds gave it serious horsepower to compensate for that. Under that long hood was a 425 cid V8 that turned out 385 hp. And that was plenty.

To avoid too much weight over the front end, the torque converter was mounted behind the engine whilst the gearbox sat under the engine's left bank.

It was an ingenious piece of engineering and laid the groundwork for the American

automobile industry's switch from rear to front-wheel drive.

The Toronado's styling was no less revolutionary. It was the work of GM design boss William L Mitchell and he really made this Olds stand out from the crowd. Boldly flared wheelarches, fenders that jutted out aggressively from the front, headlamps hidden away and a fastback tail made this one striking car.

The Toronado was a big hit in its first year of production

MODEL HISTORY

1966	1966	1968	1970	1971
Oldsmobile launches the biggest ever front-wheel drive car	Motor Trend names the Toronado Car of the Year	Restyle tames the Toronado a little	But not for long, GT launched with 400bhp	Second generation emphasizes luxury over muscle

with more than 40,000 models sold.

1968 saw the Toronado tamed a little. Those stand-out fenders were reigned in and Olds' new split grille was added, whilst under the hood a new 455 cubic inch 375bhp V8 was fitted.

1970 saw a more significant change, with fixed headlamps replacing the concealed ones and the

addition of a 400bhp GT version. With a special cam and torque converter the GT could hit zero to sixty in just seven and a half

Specification

Years built	1966-1970
Most powerful model	1970 GT
Engine type	V8
Displacement	455 cid
Transmission	three-speed automatic
Power	400bhp
Top speed	135mph

seconds. You could spot a Toronado GT thanks to its twin exhausts, slotted rear bumper and gold paintwork with black stripes.

During the five-year production run more than 120,000 series one Toronados rolled out of the factory. The series two that followed is the collectors' item. Just ask Jay Leno, he's a proud Toronado owner.

Plymouth
Barracuda

It beat the Mustang to market, but it would be some years before the 'Cuda could be considered a true pony car

A true muscle car it ain't – but the 1964 Plymouth Barracuda did beat the Mustang to market by two weeks. Its other claim to fame was its huge wrap-round rear window, said to be the largest single piece of glass ever used on a production car. Initially the Plymouth sales pitch concentrated on the Barracuda's looks and convenience and the most sporty engine on offer was a 273 cubic inch 235bhp V8.

The Formula S Barracuda, introduced in 1965, was supposed to be a performance car. But it wasn't. The most powerful engine on offer was still

Plymouth Barracuda 2-Door Sports Hardtop

1970 'Cuda (opposite page), advert for the '65 (above) and 1970 'Cuda Hemi (right)

The 273 cubic inch 235bhp V8 and it wasn't any faster than standard models. There was a facelift in 1966 and the distinctive 'Fish' badges were added.

Then, in 1967, things began to change. Notchback and convertible body styles were added to the original fastback. Plymouth even thought about adding their 280bhp 383 cubic inch engine to the options list.

A 383 cubic inch V8 was squeezed into the 1968 car and coincided with an abbreviation of the name.

The Formula S Barracuda became the sportier-sounding 'Cuda with no less than 300bhp on tap. The zero to 60mph dash was accomplished in a reasonably rapid 7.5 seconds. But, despite the power upgrade, the quarter mile was managed in the hardly competitive high 15s.

1969 saw more attempts to make the 'Cuda faster and more competitive with its rival muscle cars. On offer were the 383 V8 with 330bhp and the most powerful engine in the Plymouth stable, the 440 cubic inch, triple carb 390bhp V8 – the largest engine ever offered in a

pony car. With a weight distribution of front/rear 57/43 per cent and no room for power-steering the car was a pig to handle. However the engine helped define the 'Cudas sportier image – zero to 60 took 5.6 seconds and the quarter-mile an impressive 14.01 seconds.

The 'Cuda finally made it in 1970. It was given a new platform, the E-body shared with the new Dodge Challenger. The 'Cuda's wheelbase was two inches shorter, though its overall dimensions were the same. No less than five V8s were on offer, the most muscular being the 390bhp 440+6 and the mighty 425bhp 426 Hemi. 'Cudas with these engines had tougher performance suspension and the Hemi had a feature that quickly became a muscle car icon – the 'Shaker' hood scoop – so-called because when the engine shook, which it did a lot, so did the Shaker.

There was also a special 'Cuda for 1970 – the AAR. It was sparked by 'Cudas raced by Dan Gurney's All-America Racers in the Trans-Am races. But unlike the Boss 302 Mustang and the Camaro Z28, the AAR 'Cuda was built as a street rod. An estimated 1,500 AARs were built.

Specification

Years built	1964 to 1974
Most powerful model	1970 Hemi 'Cuda
Engine type	V8
Displacement	426 cu in
Transmission	three-speed automatic
Power	425bhp
Top speed	130mph

MODEL HISTORY

1964
Plymouth Barracuda beats Mustang to market by two weeks

1966
Barracuda fish emblems introduced. Most powerful engine has just 235bhp

1967
Notchback Barracuda joins ranks of pony cars. Performance Formula S version available

1968
383 cubic inch 300 horsepower V8 Barracuda

1969
440 cubic inch, triple carb 390 horsepower V8 is the largest engine ever offered in a pony car

Plymouth
Prowler

Plymouth's concept car made real may not have had much muscle, but its hot rod styling made it a hit

The Plymouth Prowler looks like a flight of fantasy, a concept car that has just rolled off a show podium. And basically, that's what it is. The Prowler is one of those rare beasts – a concept car that made it into production.

A modern interpretation of the street hot rods of the Fifties, the Prowler made its debut at the Detroit Auto Show of 1993. Jaws dropped, flashbulbs popped and nobody really thought that Plymouth's parent company, the Chrysler corporation, would ever

reliability and modern automobile attributes, it was a godsend.

The car was the most aluminum-intensive car produced in North America at the time. Most of the bodywork was constructed of this lightweight metal, as was the suspension, helping to reduce weight as much as possible. And it needed to keep itself trim because, unlike its spiritual forebears from the Fifties, it was notpowered by a huge V8.

The power unit was the same 3.5-liter (213 cid) V6 found in Chrysler's sedans, producing 214bhp. In the (relatively) lightweight Prowler,

2001 Prowler (opposite page and above with custom trailer) and 1999 model (below)

build it. It was just too wild. But they reckoned without Chrysler president Bob Lutz, whose support for the project was pivotal in getting the Prowler signed off and into production.

It would take until 1997, for this automobile to finally hit the street. But when it did, it remained remarkably true to its original concept. A two-seater roadster with a manually-operated soft top and the sort of radical looks only normally found at hot rod clubs, it was a unique, off-the-peg custom car. For the guy who wanted a street rod but also wanted comfort,

its performance was brisk rather than roadburning. But who cared when you were at the wheel of something this outrageous and getting all the looks?

The Prowler was given a bit more go to accompany the show when a new aluminum V6 started taking care of business in 1998. Power rose to 253bhp, making this a lively but well-mannered roadster. A four-speed Autostick transmission had manual override, allowing the driver to shift up and down the ratios by tapping a stick shift. The ride quality was firm and performance-oriented, although it would be softened down during its years of production.

Originally only available in purple, a whole slew of retro hot-rod colours gradually became available over the car's five-year lifespan. But luggage space was minimal and there wasn't even room to stow a spare tire.

The Prowler ceased production in 2002, and apart from the original engine being upgraded, few major changes were made to the model during its life cycle.

It remained the dream machine that inspired so many auto enthusiasts to take it to their hearts.

Specification

Years built	1997 to 2002
Most powerful model	1998 onwards
Engine type	V6
Displacement	213 cu in
Transmission	four-speed Autostick
Power	253bhp
Top speed	125mph

MODEL HISTORY

1993
Prowler is first displayed at Detroit and rocks the show

1994
Prototype is taken to hot rod shows to gauge reaction

1996
Official go-ahead for the model is announced at Detroit

1997
First production Prowlers built alongside the Dodge Viper

1998
All-aluminum 3.5-liter (214 cid) V6 introduced, giving 253bhp

1999

New shock absorbers and springs give a smoother ride

1999

Black and red two-tone Woodward Edition unveiled. Only 150 made

2000

Black Tie silver an black special edition released. Only 163 made

2001

Plymouth brand is discontinued, Prowler is rebadged as a Chrysler

2002

The Prowler cruises off into the sunset as the model is axed

2001(above)
and 1999
(right)

1998 model (above) and 1997 (right)

Plymouth
Road Runner

*The back-to-basics Plymouth Road Runner was one
of the most successful muscle cars ever. Beep Beep!*

When the Road Runner hit the
scene in 1968, it made the biggest
impact on the market since
Pontiac's GTO back in '64. Four
years of muscle car development

had resulted in expensive, luxury-
laden automobiles, so with the
Road Runner, Plymouth decided
to get back to base principals.

For a mere $2,896, the

American public could purchase a
base-level Road Runner, equipped
with a 383 cubic inch V8
pumping out 335bhp. The
chassis, based on the Plymouth

paid Warner Brothers a reported $50,000 to use their famously fast cartoon bird as the car's logo – and adopted its name too. To go with the decals, there was even a horn that went "beep-beep" in cartoon Road Runner style.

Just like its animated namesake, the car was a runaway success. Plymouth expected to sell 2,500 in its first year, but pretty soon it was the car every kid wanted and 45,000 flew out of the dealerships.

1970 Super Bird (opposite page), 1969 (above) and 1974 Road Runner (below)

Belvedere, was beefed up with uprated suspension, while the interior was right back to basics with a simple bench seat and rubber matting replacing carpets.

It was an impressive package for the price, but for an extra $714 you could put a fearsome 426 Hemi under the hood of your Road Runner. For just $3,610 you could own an automobile that could do 0-60mph in 5.3 seconds and tear up a quarter-mile in the low 13s.

And what a cool car! Plymouth created the perfect youth-oriented image for its new creation. The company

133

MUSCLE CARS

Its success prompted Plymouth to expand the range in 1969, bringing in a convertible to bolster the existing hardtop and pillared coupe. Two new 440 cid V8s included the "440 + 6", a triple-carb job which gave Hemi-like acceleration for almost half the price.

Another feature with hip graphics gave the Road Runner a psychological edge. In 1970, the Air Grabber Hood appeared on the options list. A powered trap door on the hood popped up when operated by a dashboard switch revealing a shark cartoon and the words "Air Grabber". A cool way to demoralize the opposition at the stoplight!

NASCAR rules required car makers to build one car per dealer for it to be eligible for the race series and Plymouth ended up making nearly 2,000 Super Birds. But despite success on the track, 1970 remained the only year it was produced.

The next year saw a stripping-down of the Road Runner range. The Hemi was legislated out of existence and the two-door hardtop was the only body style on offer.

The end came in 1980, with the final Plymouth Road Runner.

Specification

Years built	1968 to 1980
Most powerful model	1970 Hemi Super Bird
Engine type	V8
Displacement	426 cu in
Transmission	four-speed manual
Power	425bhp
Top speed	160mph

MODEL HISTORY

1968
First Road Runner is a very animated package offering big bangs for low bucks

1969
Range expanded with two new V8s and a convertible added to the line-up

1969
Road Runner sales double

1970
Air grabber hood offered as an option

1970
Ultimate Road Runner, the Super Bird, is created with race-oriented aero styling

The star of 1970, Plymouth Road Runner Super Bird

Pontiac
Firebird

From Smokey and the Bandit to Knight Rider the Pontiac Firebird Trans Am was an American hero for 35 years

The Firebird has a special place in the history of American performance vehicles. The story started in 1967, when the first Firebird's distinctly beaky hood and GTO-style tail lights successfully established a separate identity to the Chevrolet Camaro that it was based on. Initially available with six different engines, most buyers went for the V8s which included the 400 cubic inch, 325bhp unit from Pontiac's GTO.

The power peak came in 1970, with the Ram Air V, a special-order 440 cubic-inch motor kicking out 500bhp. The engine formed part of the Firebird's top performance package – called the Trans Am, after the US race series. The name would become an American automobile legend.

engine was rated by the company at 310bhp, although experts agreed it actually produced nearer 370.

When the Firebird Trans Ams which packed these fearsome engines received a new decal, their iconic status was sealed. A huge image of an eagle with its wings outspread took up most of the hood, it screamed a rallying cry to performance car fans throughout the US, giving the Trans Am massive credibility and

First (opposite page) and last (above) of the line and 1976 Trans Am (below)

The collapse of the muscle car market led GM bosses to consider axing the Firebird, but Pontiac fought to save the 'bird and it won a reprieve. It was a corporate decision that was to provide big rewards.

The Firebird blasted away the clouds with its new Super Duty 455 cubic inch V8. "Super Duty" was the name given to Pontiac's race-ready engines in the Sixties and the Super Duty 455 made the Firebird the only serious performance car on the market. This street-legal, race-prepped

MUSCLE CARS

supercool status.

As the Seventies wore on, however, further power restrictions took their toll, with the Super Duty engine phased out in '75 and the 455 V8 falling by the wayside in '76. Despite the drop in maximum power, the Firebird still managed to score sales of over 100,000 for the first time in 1976. A serious boost for the car's image came the next year, when Burt Reynolds drove a black and gold Special Edition Trans Am in the hit movie Smokey and the Bandit. Another starring role reaffirmed the Firebird's popularity in 1982, when it got all the best lines performing as "KITT", David Hasselhoff's talking techno-car in Knight Rider.

The third-generation, hatchback-bodied 'bird now saw a gradual increase in output. 1987 saw a new 210bhp 350 cid V8 and in '89 a 250bhp turbocharged V6 powered the special 20th anniversary edition Trans Am.

The final generation, from 1993-2002, were the fastest and most powerful. Top dog was a 5.7-liter V8 which developed from 275 to 320bhp during 1993-98. But the model didn't live long into the 21st century.

Specification

Years built	1967 to 2002
Most powerful model	1970 Ram Air V
Engine type	V8
Displacement	400 cu in
Transmission	three-speed automatic
Power	500bhp
Top speed	130mph

MODEL HISTORY

1967
First Firebird, based on the Camaro chassis from Pontiac's fellow GM brand, Chevrolet

1969
'Trans Am' first introduced as a performance package. It becomes symbolic of Pontiac muscle

1970
Second-generation 'bird gets the 500bhp Ram Air V engine as an optional power unit

1973
Golden Eagle spreads its wings on the Trans Am's hood

1976
The Firebird ceases to pack 455 V8 power

1976

Not that it stops people buying. Firebird sales hit 100,000 in one year

1977

Burt Reynolds makes the car a star, driving a Trans Am in Smokey and the Bandit

1982

Third-generation Firebird stars as "KITT" in the hit TV show, Knight Rider

1993

The final generation Firebird is unveiled

2002

The Firebird celebrates its 35th anniversary... but then its wings are clipped

Trans Ams from 1967 (above) and 1971 (right)

Pontiac Grand Prix

The least extrovert of Pontiac's muscle cars still offered plenty of performance

Although tastefully low-key in styling, the Pontiac Grand Prix sported a good few muscle car credentials in its launch year of 1962. Not least was the special build of 16 cars equipped with the 421 cubic inch 370bhp Super Duty V8 that took the Grand Prix to 60 miles an hour in a respectable 6.6 seconds. Just one of these specials is believed to survive. Otherwise muscle car fans made do with the 425-A Trophy V8 engines and a maximum output of 348bhp.

The Grand Prix's interior was fairly sporty with bucket seats, floor shift, and an instrument console with a tachometer. Chequered flag badges front and

Following the Detroit trend, the Grand Prix got bigger and heavier for its next incarnation in 1965. A bench seat was on offer to replace the original bucket seats and console. Power actually increased with new engine features such as better gas flow through new design manifolds and cylinder heads. The 389 base engine had 256bhp and Tri-Power version increased this to 338. The 421 four-barrel carb also made 338bhp and the two Tri-Power engines put this figure up to 353 and 376bhp respectively.

1965 in Paris (opposite page), 1971 (above) and 1962 (below)

rear gave a nod to the car's name and race aspirations.

The Grand Prix was given a new look for 1963. An unusual concave rear window gave the car a very distinctive profile. The rear window was to stay as a Grand Prix feature until the 1968 model year. The high power engines for 1963 were two 421 cubic inch V8s, one with a four-barrel carb that put out 353bhp – the other was a 370bhp version called the HO Tri-Power. The 1963 car proved to be popular with car buyers with a total of nearly 73,000 sold.

MUSCLE CARS

The beginning of the end for this generation of the Grand Prix came in 1966 as sales of the manual transmission cars fell to under 1,000.

The Grand Prix got even bigger in 1967, and it was the only year a convertible version was on offer. The car now looked massive and to cope with the increased weight the base engine was now a 400 cubic inch V8 with 350bhp. The most powerful V8 was the 421 cubic inch engine which put out 376bhp. 1967 was also the year that exhaust emissions had to meet Federal smog regulations, and the introduction of first-phase safety equipment. The Grand Prix now came with a collapsible steering wheel, dual-circuit hydraulics and optional disc brakes. But the car's size now put off buyers and sales continued to fall.

It wasn't until another re-design in 1969 that the buying public took to the Pontiac Grand Prix in reasonable numbers. The wheelbase was three inches shorter. The car handled better and with its new 428 cubic inch 390 horsepower V8 it ran the all-important quarter-mile in 14.1 seconds.

Specification

Years built	1962 to 1974
Most powerful model	1968
Engine type	V8
Displacement	428 cu in
Transmission	three-speed automatic
Power	390bhp
Top speed	129mph

MODEL HISTORY

1962
Pontiac Grand Prix introduced with 425-A Trophy V8 engines and a maximum output of 348bhp

1963
Re-style with lower roofline and concave rear window

1963
Sales of 73,000 prove re-styled car's popularity

1965
The 421 Tri-Power engines put out 353 and 376 bhp respectively

1966
Sales of manual transmission cars fall to under 1,000

Pontiac GTO

In many eyes the Pontiac GTO was the first true muscle car with full-size power in its mid-size shell

This is where it all began. In 1964 Pontiac saw a gap in the market. The mid-size market was down on performance and prestige as a result of a GM ban on factory-backed racing and a limit of 330 cubic inches on standard engine size.

In a cunning move Pontiac got around these restrictions by offering the LeMans GTO (Gran Turismo Omologato) package as an option on the Tempest model.

It was distinguished from the regular Tempest thanks to air scoops on the hood, special redline tires, heavy duty suspension, three-speed floor-shift tranny, chromed air cleaner and rocker cover and a special 'engine-turned' instrument panel plate.

With a 389 cubic inch V8 from the Bonneville under the hood, the GTO offered 325bhp in standard trim. The Tri-Power kit replaced the standard four barrel carburator with three double-barrel carbs and upped that power to 348bhp.

could now be used to feed a ram air system that could be bought from dealers.

A year later and the GTO became a model in its own right. There was yet another restyle to give the car a more sculptured Coke bottle look, but there were no changes under the hood.

By 1967 GM had banned multiple carburators on all models except the Chevrolet Corvette, so Pontiac needed

1968 coupe and convertible (opposite), 1965 (above) and 1964 (below) two- doors

With a 0-60mph time of 7.5 seconds and able to run the standing quarter-mile in les than 15 seconds the GTO quickly gained legendary status. Sales went through the roof. Pontiac hoped to sell 5,000 in the first year, but in the event more than 32,000 found owners. This car was a sensation.

For '65 Pontiac capitalised on the astonishing success of the GTO with a major front and rear restyle. The bonnet scoops that were just styling ploys on the '64 model

MUSCLE CARS

another solution. In went a bored-out 400 cid V8 that came in four states of tune. There was Economy with just 255bhp, Standard with 335bhp or HO (High Output) and Ram Air, both with 360bhp.

The GTO was restyled once again for 1968 and sat on a new 112-inch wheelbase. The innovative rubber Endura bumper was now fitted and hidden headlamps were added to the options list. The Economy and Standard engines both gained 10bhp but the HO and Ram Air stayed at 360bhp.

1969 was the year of the Judge. This special edition GTO was named after a phrase on TV's 'Laugh In' this GTO featured wild paint colors and a hefty rear spoiler. Two new Ram Air engines offered 366 and 370bhp. The GTO was getter faster by the year.

The coolest trick of 1970 was the VOE option. This Vacuum Operated Exhaust system employed a hot rod technique that opened the exhaust to give more power. Over the next three years the GTO suffered like all GM muscle cars with restrictions on horsepower and emissions.

The GTO is a true modern muscle car and not just a namesake.

Specification

Years built	1965 to 1974, 2004 to date
Most powerful model	2005 GTO
Engine type	V8
Displacement	364 cu in
Transmission	six-speed manual
Power	400bhp
Top speed	150mph

MODEL HISTORY

1964 Pontiac fits a Bonneville engine in the Tempest, creating the GTO

1965 First restyle and power increased to 360bhp with the Tri-Power option

1966 GTO becomes a model in its own right

1967 Multiple carbs banned, new 400 cid V8 installed

1968 Another restyle features indestructible Endura bumpers

1969

The year of the
Judge – the
wildest-looking
GTO yet

1970

Sneaky VOE option
makes GTO faster
syill, but annoys
GM bosses

1971

Horsepower rates
reduced to meet
tough emissions
rules

1974

GTO production
ceases

2004

A legend lives
on with new
400bhp GTO

1964 convertible (above) and 1970 coupe (right)

1967 convertible (above) and 1974 coupe (left)

Shelby *Cobra*

When Carroll Shelby teamed American V8 power with a lightweight British sports car he created a legend that still lives on today

Created by one of the most charismatic characters in American sportscar history, the Cobra has attained mythical status amongst automobile fans the world over. Larger-than-life Texan Carroll Shelby was the man who synthesised US muscle and English style so perfectly that the car is still built today – over 40 years after its original inception.

Shelby, a successful sportscar racer and previous winner of prestigious European endurance race, the Le Mans 24 Hours, was forced to retire from the track in 1960 due to ill-health. With a vision of producing a sportscar combining a lightweight European chassis

1962 (opposite), 1964 Le Mans (above) and 1964 road car (below)

months in early 1962, the cute little Ace was transformed into a hair-raising beast at Shelby's California workshop. What emerged was a classic expression of muscularity in metal – the original Cobra roadster, the fastest production car ever made at that time. With explosive acceleration from 0-60mph in a breath-taking 3.9 seconds, the car won rave reviews from motoring journalists and its curvaceous lines wowed the crowds at American auto shows. Shelby's visionary concept had struck a major chord in the hearts of

with American V8 power, he set about making his dream a reality. The opportunity came the next year, when English manufacturer AC cars agreed to Shelby's idea of muscling-up its Ace sportscar, and a deal was struck.

Luckily for the Texan, Ford had just developed a new small-block V8 but had no serious performance model to put it in. After successful negotiations, the recipe was written for one of the most spine-tingling sportscars ever made.

During a couple of

sportscar fans.

The first Cobra packed a 256 cubic inch engine, but its creator's insatiable desire for power and performance meant that pretty soon a 289 cubic-inch version of the Ford V8 was installed. And it didn't stop there. Shelby campaigned the Cobra successfully in American and European race series – and it was his desire to win that produced

the most awesome Cobra of all.

Deciding to shoehorn an even bigger Ford V8 under the hood to keep it competitive in production endurance racing, Shelby went for the 427 cubic-inch option. By 1967, 31 competition cars equipped with this engine had been finished – not enough to qualify the model for racing. His only option was to fit windscreens to unsold Cobras

that had already been built and offer them for sale to the general public in order to meet the quota.

The 427 Cobra was born – one of the fastest-accelerating production cars of its day, with vital statistics of 0-60mph in 4.5 seconds, a standing quarter-mile in 12.4 and 165mph top speed. That's blisteringly quick, even by today's standards!

Specification

Years built	1962 to date
Most powerful model	1965 427
Engine type	V8
Displacement	427 cu in
Transmission	four-speed manual
Power	410bhp
Top speed	165mph

MODEL HIS

1960
Carroll Shelby retires from racing with a dream to build the ultimate sportscar

1962
First ... built ... Ace ... Ford ...

Cobra ... Coupe ... class at ... Hours

1965
The 427, featuring ... frame and ... aluminium body is unveiled

1967
427 available
to the public

1967
The last 427
Cobra is built

1989
Shelby begins his
427 Cobra S/C
project, finishing
"leftover" cars
from the Sixties

1995
CSX4000-series
427 Cobra S/C
Roadsters
are built

2005
Shelby's company
continues to
build Cobras
to order

1965 Cobras for road and track (above and right)

*1969 289s
(above and left)*